CONFIGURING CASH AND BANK MANAGEMENT WITHIN DYNAMICS AX 2012

BY MURRAY FIFE

Preface

What You Need For This Guide

All the examples shown in this blueprint were done with the Microsoft Dynamics AX 2012 virtual machine image that was downloaded from the Microsoft CustomerSource or PartnerSource site. If you don't have your own installation of Microsoft Dynamics AX 2012, you can also use the images found on the Microsoft Learning Download Center or deployed through Lifecycle Services. The following list of software from the virtual image was leveraged within this guide:

- Microsoft Dynamics AX 2012 R3

Even though all the preceding software was used during the development and testing of the recipes in this book, they may also work on earlier versions of the software with minor tweaks and adjustments, and should also work on later versions without any changes.

Errata

Although we have taken every care to ensure the accuracy of our content, mistakes do happen. If you find a mistake in one of our books—maybe a mistake in the text or the code—we would be grateful if you would report this to us. By doing so, you can save other readers from frustration and help us improve subsequent versions of this book. If you find any errata, please report them by emailing editor@dynamicsaxcompanions.com.

Piracy

Piracy of copyright material on the Internet is an ongoing problem across all media. If you come across any illegal copies of our works, in any form, on the Internet, please provide us with the location address or website name immediately so that we can pursue a remedy.

Please contact us at legal@dynamicsaxcompanions.com with a link to the suspected pirated material.

We appreciate your help in protecting our authors, and our ability to bring you valuable content.

Questions

You can contact us at help@dynamicsaxcompanions.com if you are having a problem with any aspect of the book, and we will do our best to address it.

Table Of Contents

CONFIGURING ADVANCED BANK RECONCILIATION (Ctd)

INTRODUCTION

Although the Cash And Bank Management module is not the most glamorous of the different areas within Dynamics AX, but it is important if you want to manage all of your bank accounts and make sure that you can easily reconcile your bank accounts. With additional features though like the ability to configure Positive Pay, this module isn't as mild mannered as you would think.

In this book we will show how to configure your Cash And Bank Management module so that you can start tracking cash and bank transactions and even streamline the process through the Bank Reconciliation features and Positive Pay within Dynamics AX.

CONFIGURING BANK MANAGEMENT CONTROLS

Before we can start setting up our Banks Accounts, there is a little bit of setup that we need to do in order to set up all of the codes and controls. We need to configure our bank transaction types that we will want to use, create a few reason codes and also check out parameters and posting profiles.

In this chapter we will step you through the initial configuration of the Cash and Bank Management so that everything is ready for you.

Configuring The Bank Transaction Types

Later on as we set up additional modules like Accounts Payable and Accounts Receivable, we will be asked to specify the **Bank Transaction Type Code** that is associated with the payment and receipt transactions. So now is a good time to get ahead of the curve and set them up.

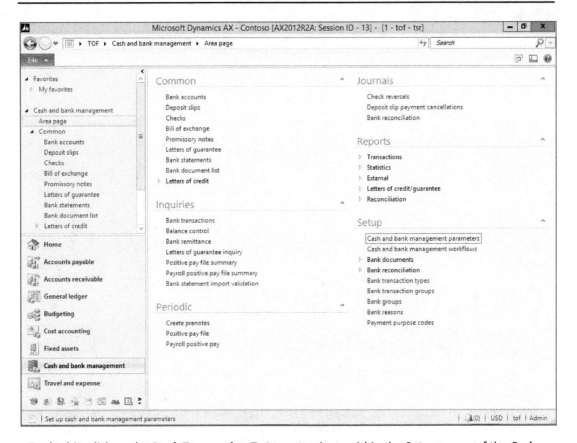

To do this, click on the **Bank Transaction Types** menu item within the **Setup** group of the **Cash And Bank Management** area page.

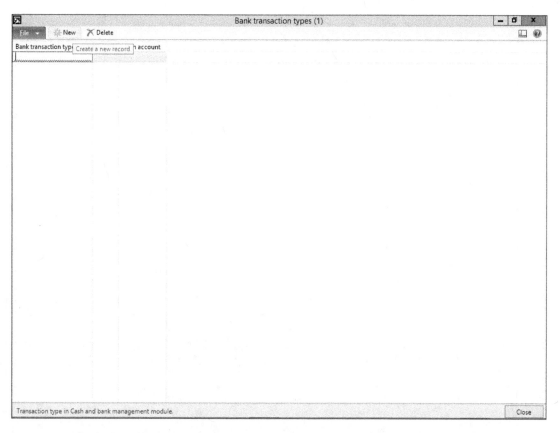

When the **Bank Transaction Types** maintenance form is displayed, click on the **New** button in the menu bar to create a new record.

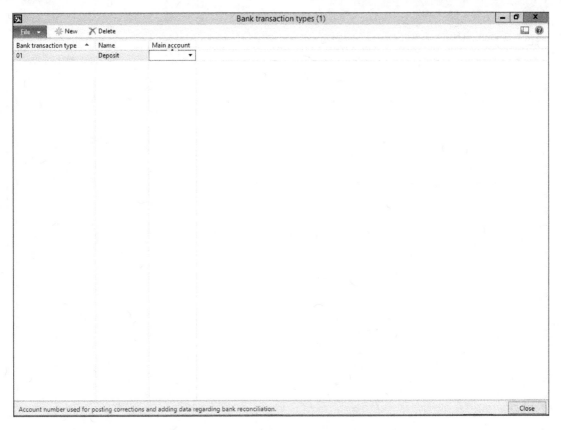

Then assign your new record a **Bank Transaction Type** code, and a name.

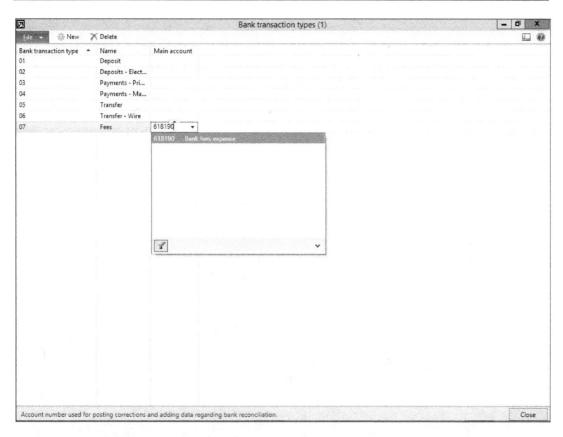

Keep on adding **Bank Transaction Types**.

If you cone across a **Bank Transaction Type** that you want to post to a specific account code then you can also override the default by specifying it in the **Main Account** field.

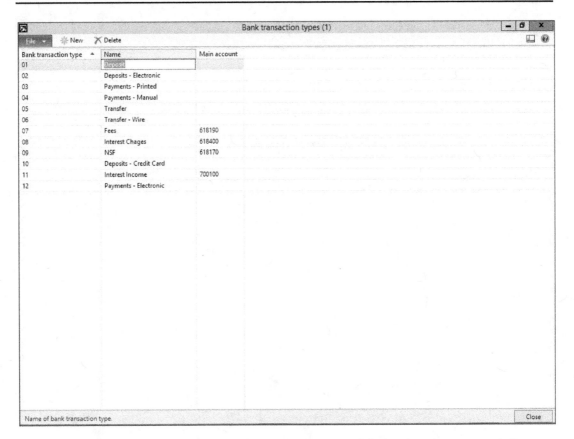

After you have added all of the **Bank Transaction Types** just click the **Close** button to exit from the form.

Configuring Bank Transaction Groups

If you want to add a little bit more structure to you **Bank Transaction Codes** then you can do that by grouping them within **Bank Transaction Groups** where you assign a parent code to all of the common codes. This is a good idea because it allows you to have another way of reporting out all of your bank transactions.

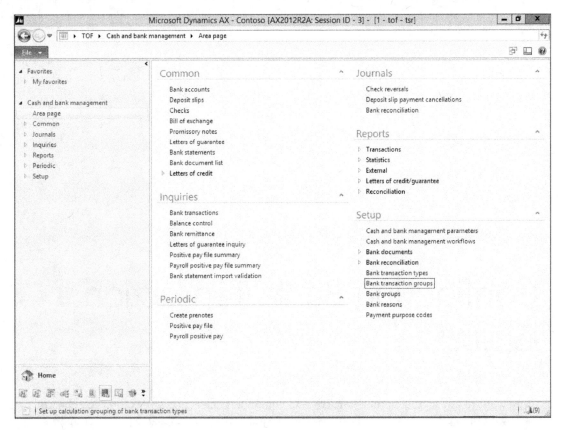

To do this click on the **Bank Transaction Groups** menu item within the **Setup** group of the **Cash and Bank Management** area page.

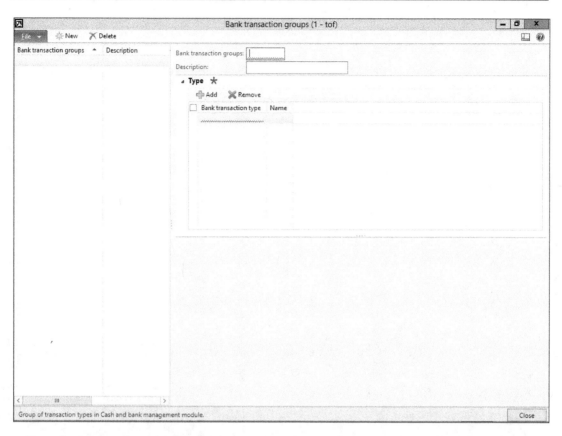

When the **Bank Transaction Groups** maintenance form is displayed click on the **New** button in the menu bar to create a new record.

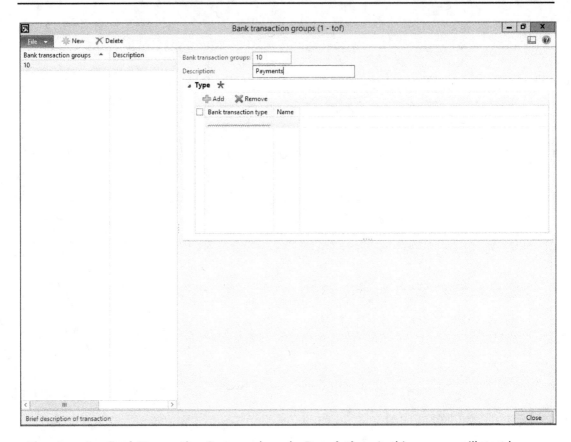

Then type in a **Bank Transaction Group** code and a **Description**. In this case we will start by creating a **Payments** group with the code of **10**.

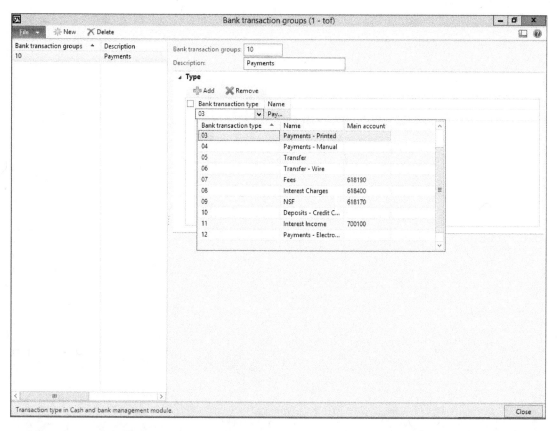

Now click on the **Add** button within the **Type** tab group and click on the **Bank Transaction Type** dropdown list to select a transaction type **03** to add to the group.

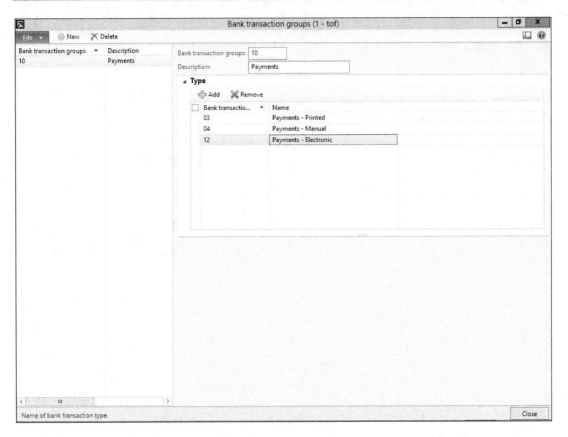

Repeat the process for all of the other transaction types that you want to add to the group which are **04** and **05**.

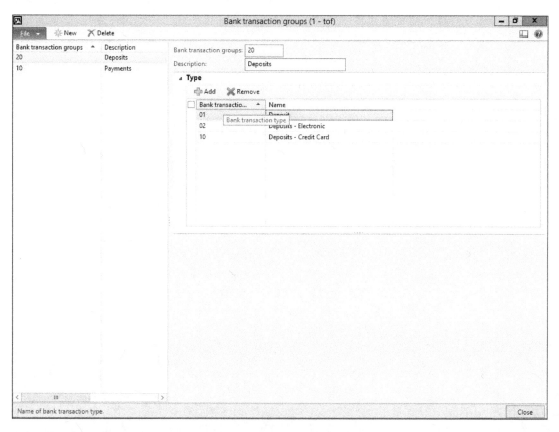

Now click on the **New** button in the menu bar to create a new group for **Deposits** with the code of **20**. Then add the transaction types **01**, **02**, and **10** to the group.

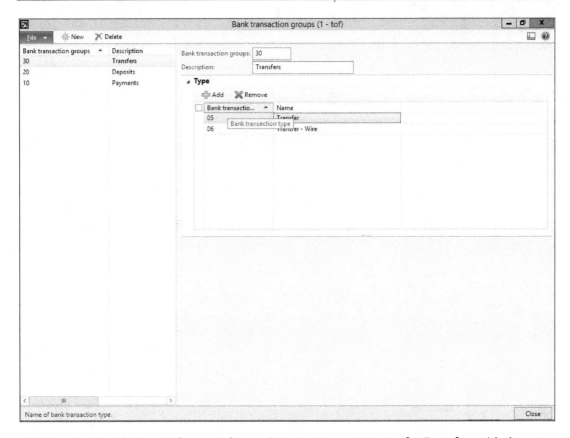

Click on the **New** button in the menu bar again to create a new group for **Transfers** with the code of **30**. Then add the transaction types **05**, and **06** to the group.

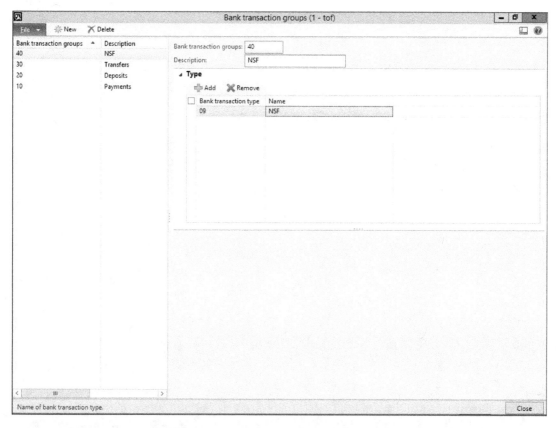

Click on the **New** button in the menu bar to create a new group for **NSF** with the code of **40**. Then add the transaction type **09** to the group.

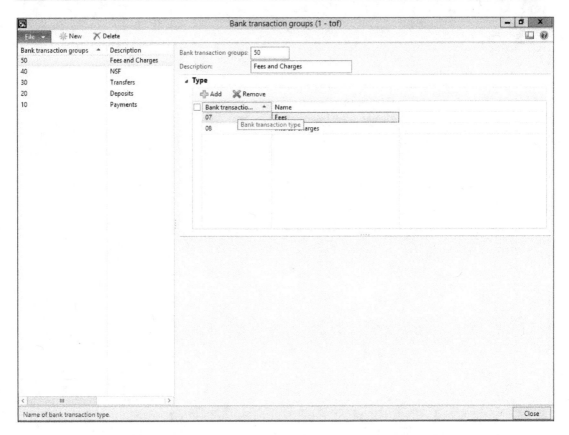

Click on the **New** button in the menu bar once more to create a new group for **Fees and Charges** with the code of **50** and add the transaction types **07**, and **08** to the group.

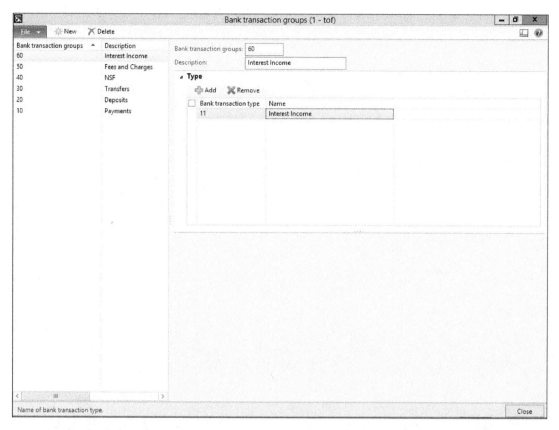

Finally click on the **New** button in the menu bar to create a new group for **Interest Income** with the code of **60**. Then add the transaction type **11** to the group.

Once you have done that, click on the **Close** button to exit from the form.

Configuring Bank Reason Codes

Just like in the General Ledger, the **Cash and Bank Management** area has reason codes that we can configure to use to track changes and adjustments. So the next step in the process is to add a few and enable them within the **Cash and Bank Management** area.

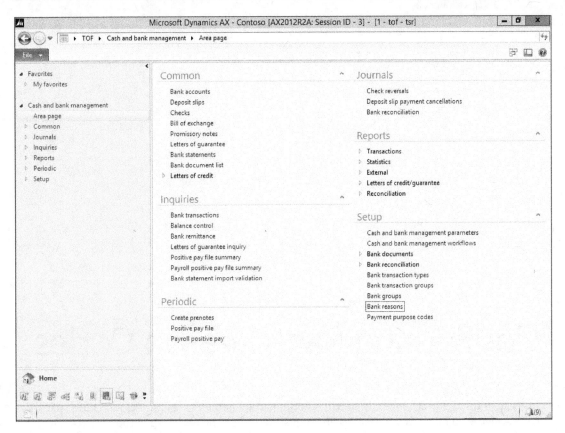

To do this, click on the **Bank Reasons** menu item within the **Setup** group of the **Cash and Bank Management** area page.

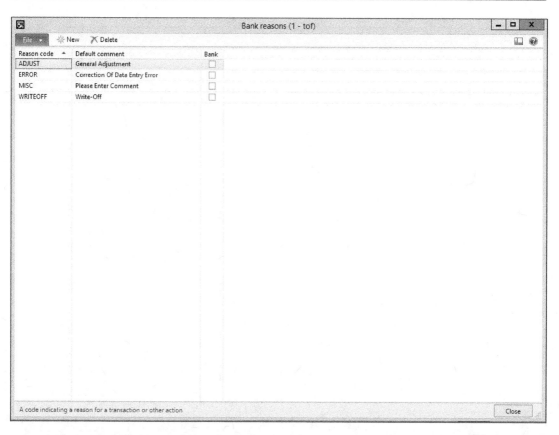

When the **Bank Reason Codes** list page is displayed you will notice that the other **Reason Codes** that you have already set up are displayed, allowing you to reuse them for the Cash and Bank Management area as well just by checking the **Bank** flag.

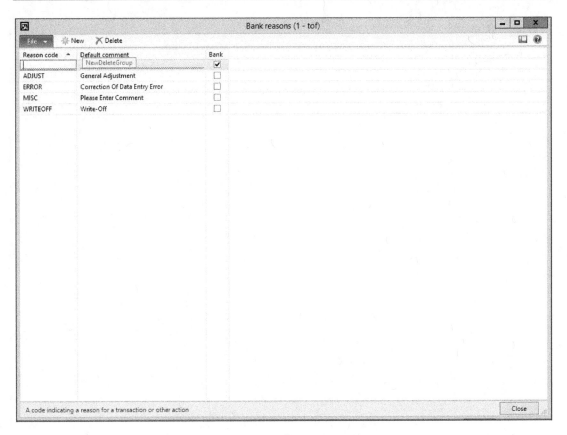

Click on the **New** button in the menu bar to create a new record.

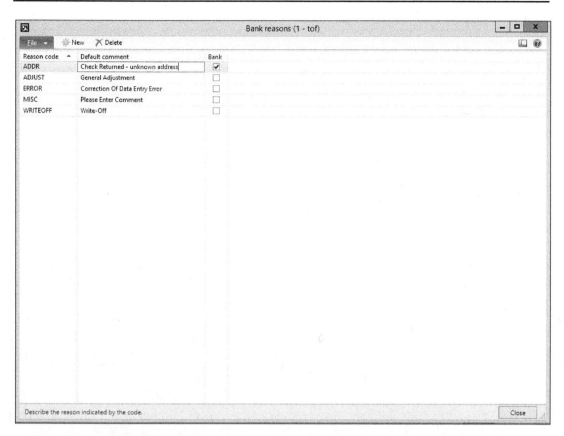

Give your new **Bank Reason** a **Reason Code**, a **Default Comment** and also make sure that the **Bank** flag is checked. For the first record we will create a Reason Code of **ADDR** with a Default Comment of **Check returned – Unknown address**.

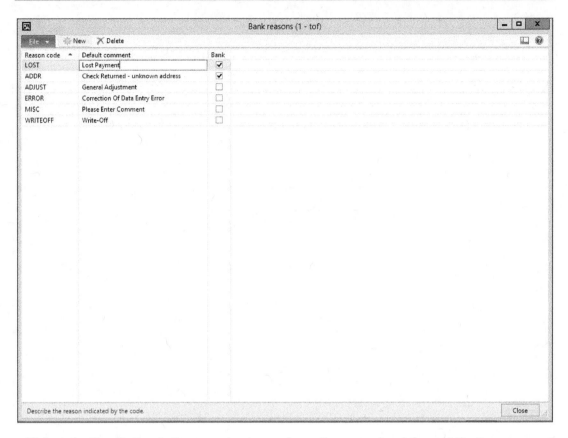

Click on the **New** button in the menu bar to create another record and then set the Reason
Code to **LOST** with a Default Comment of **Lost Payment**.

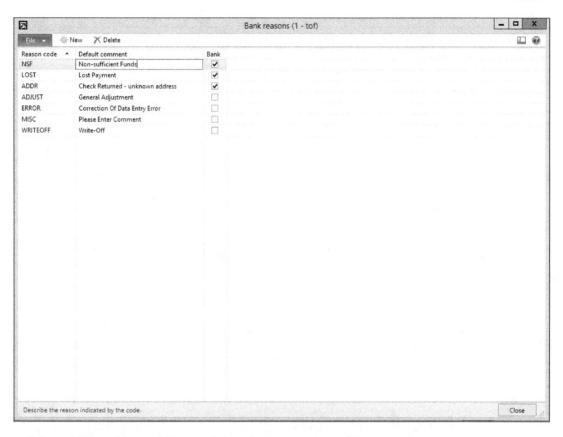

Click on the **New** button in the menu bar again to create another record and then set the Reason Code to **NSF** with a Default Comment of **Non-sufficient Funds**.

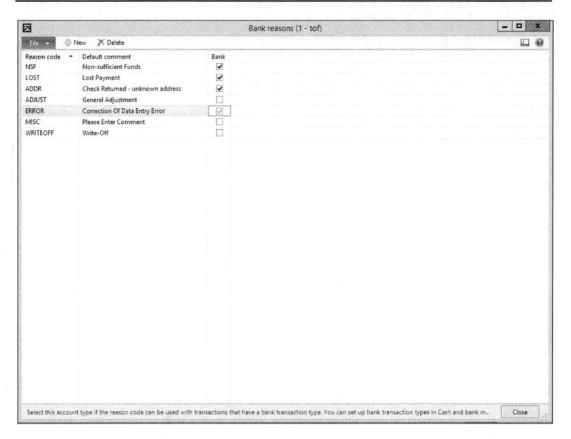

Click on the **New** button in the menu bar again to create one last record and then set the Reason Code to **ERROR** with a Default Comment of **Correction of Data Entry Error**.

When you have done that, click on the **Close** button to exit from the form.

Configuring Bank Document Posting Profiles

We can also save a lot of time within the **Cash and Bank Management** area by configuring some of the default accounts that will be posted to by configuring the **Bank Document Posting Profiles**. These will be used as reference accounts when Dynamics AX tries to post journals.

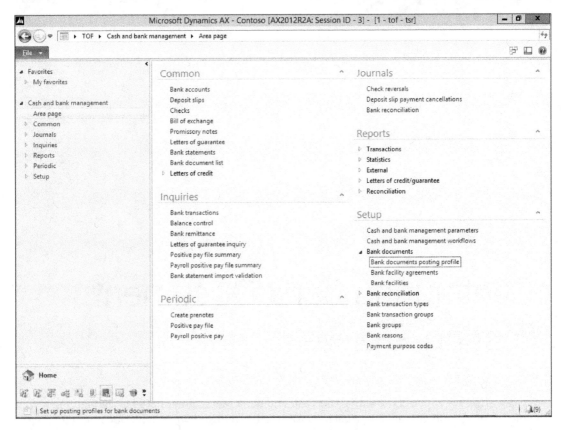

To do this, click on the **Bank Document Posting Profile** menu item within the **Bank Documents** folder of the **Setup** group within the **Cash and Bank Management** area page.

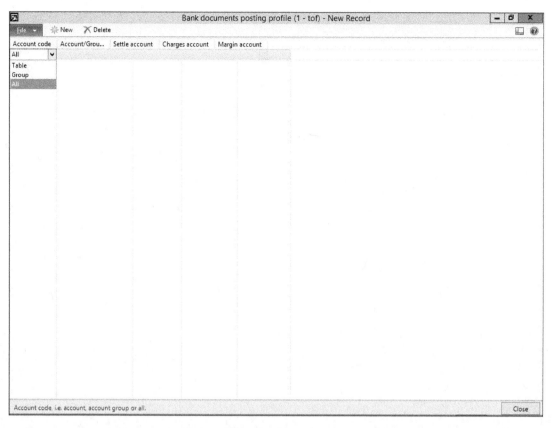

When the **Bank Document Posting Profiles** list page is displayed, click on the **New** button to create a new record and then click on the **Account Code** dropdown list. We will initially just create a global posting profile so we will select the **All** option.

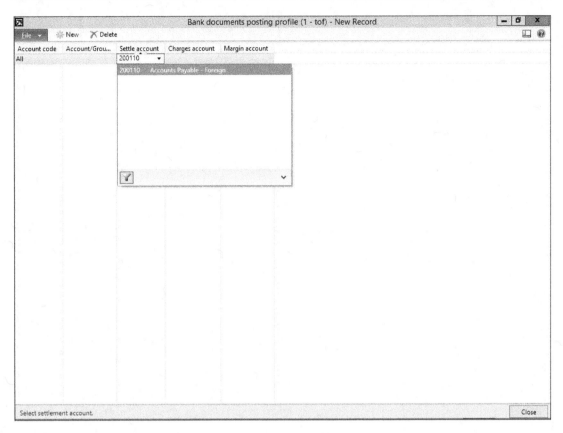

Click on the **Settle Account** dropdown list and select a GL account that we want to use as our default settlement account. We will use **200110**.

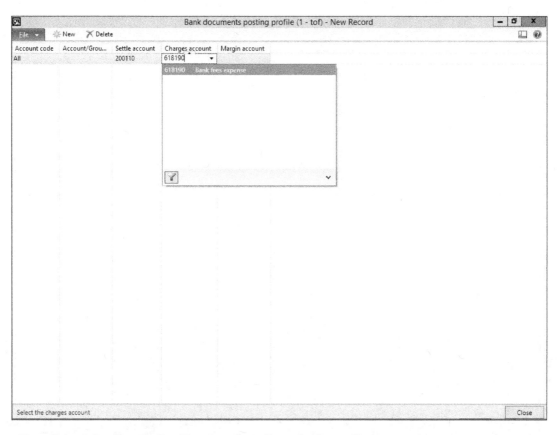

Now click on the **Charges Account** dropdown list and select a GL account that we want to use as our default account for bank charges and fees. We will use **618190**.

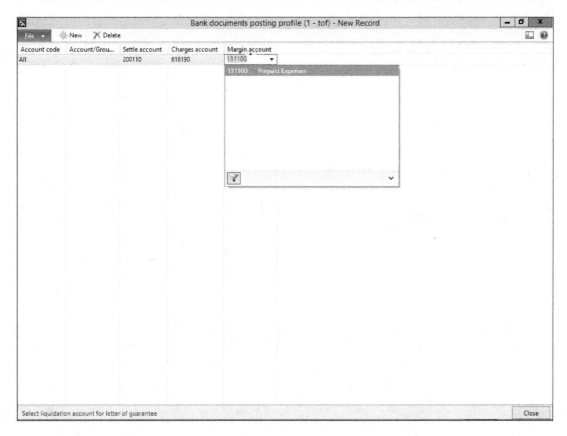

Then click on the **Margin Account** dropdown list and select a GL account that we want to use as our default account for margins. We will use **131100**.

When you have done that just click on the **Close** button to exit from the form.

Configuring Cash & Bank Management Parameters

To finish of the initial setup you may want to tweak some of the **Cash And Bank Management** parameters.

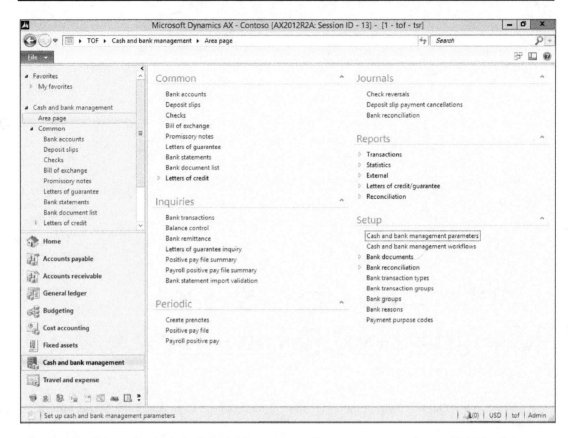

To do this, click on the **Cash And Bank Management Parameters** menu item within the **Setup** group of the **Cash And Bank Management** area page.

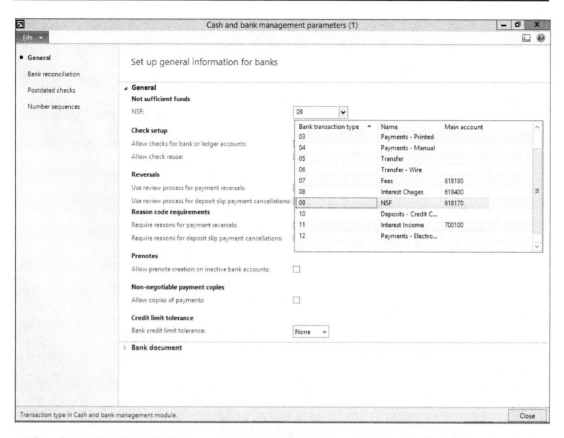

When the **Cash And Bank Management Parameters** maintenance form is displayed, select the
NSF Bank Transaction Type from the dropdown list.

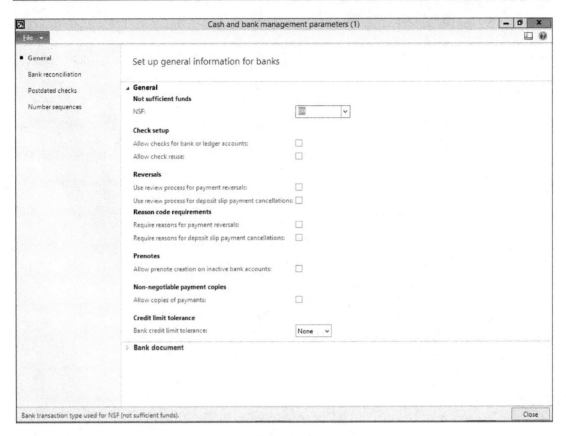

And then just click the **Close** button to exit from the form.

CONFIGURING BANK ACCOUNTS

The first area that we will look at within the **Cash Management** module is the configuration of your **Bank Accounts** so that you can start using them within your organization and later on link them to your receivables and payables functions.

Configuring Bank Groups

If you have multiple bank accounts that within the same financial institution then you might want to configure the **Bank Groups** so that you can group them all together. You can use these to track common attributes like the Routing Numbers and also use them to manage shared features such as reconciliation.

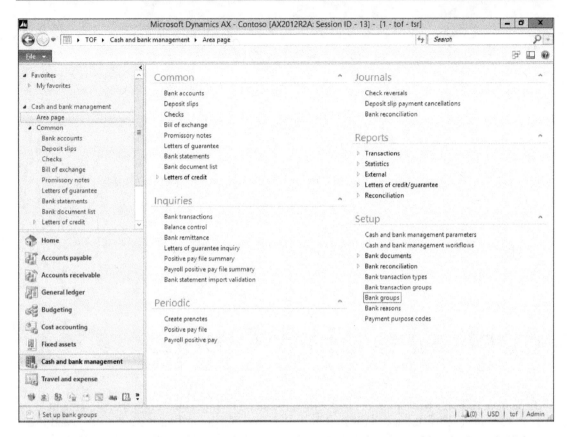

To do this, click on the **Bank Groups** menu item within the **Setup** group of the **Cash And Bank Management** area page.

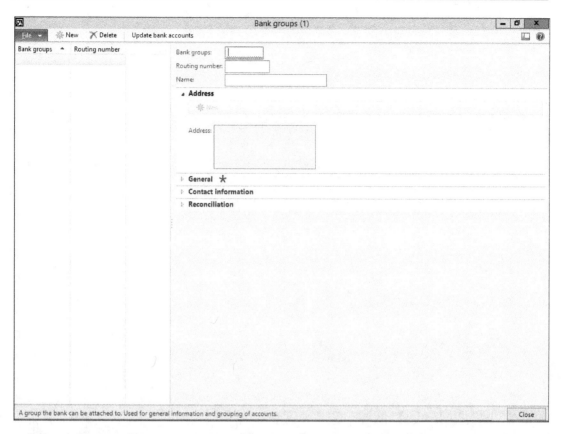

When the **Bank Groups** maintenance form is displayed, click on the **New** button in the menu bar to create a new record.

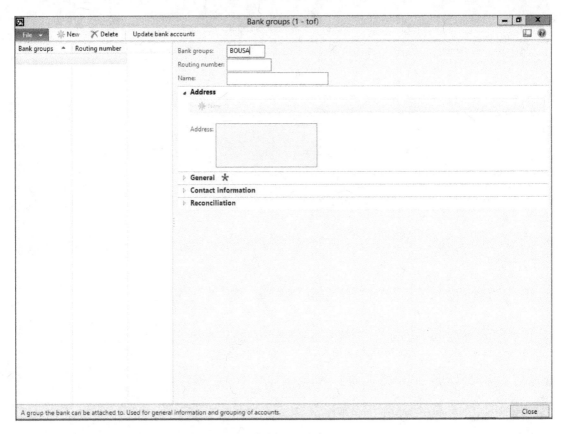

Assign your new record a **Bank Group** code of **BOUSA**

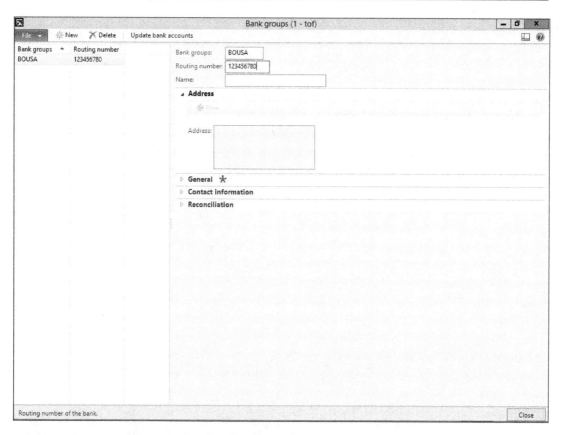

Then set the Routing Number for the group of banks.

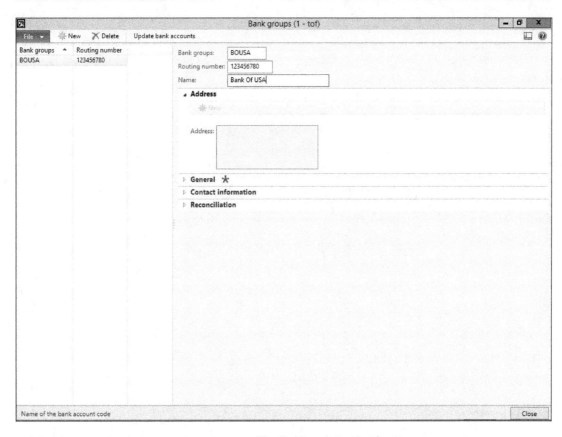

Then give your **Bank Group** a **Name**. We will call this one **Bank Of USA**.

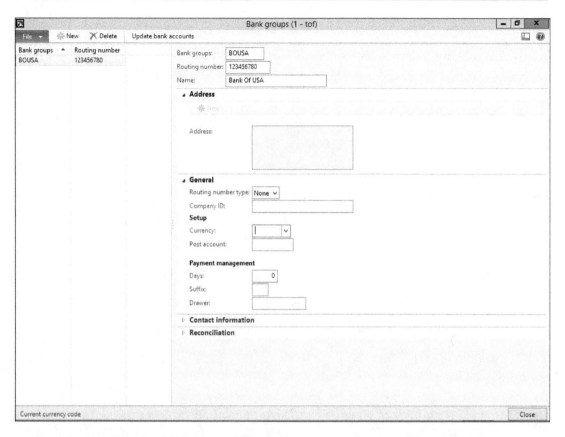

Expand the **General** tab within the **Bank Groups** form to access some additional fields.

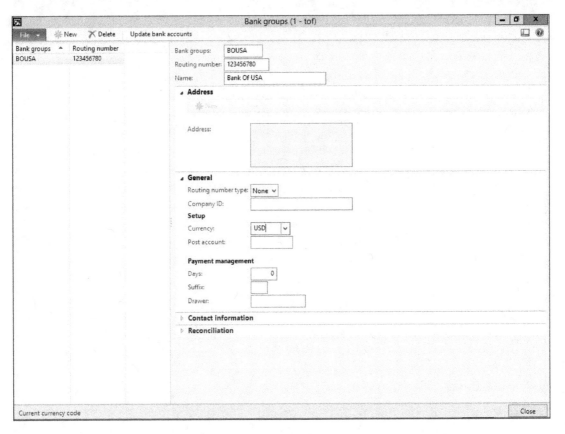

This will allow you to set the default **Currency** code for the **Bank Group** to **USD**.

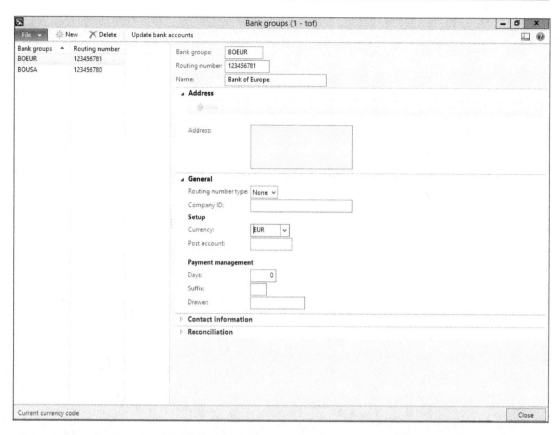

Now click on the **New** button in the menu bar to create a new record and set the **Bank Group** code to **BOEUR**, the **Routing Number** to **123456781**, the **Name** to **Bank of Europe** and the **Currency** to **EUR**.

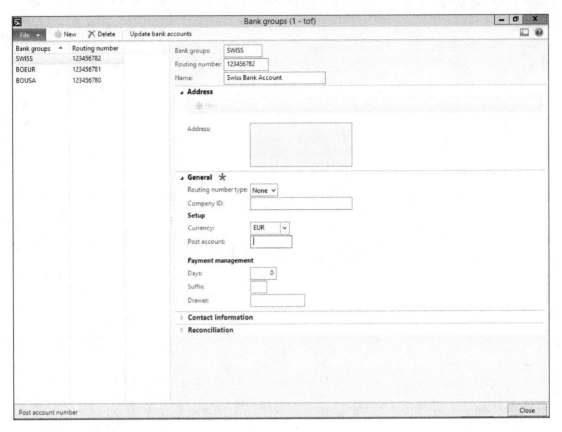

Click on the **New** button in the menu bar one more time to create another record and set the **Bank Group** code to **SWISS**, the **Routing Number** to **123456782**, the **Name** to **Swiss Bank Accounts** and the **Currency** to **EUR**.

You can continue adding **Bank Groups** and when you are done, just click the **Close** button to exit from the form.

Configuring Bank Accounts

Once you have configured your Bank Groups, then it is on to configuring your **Bank Accounts**.

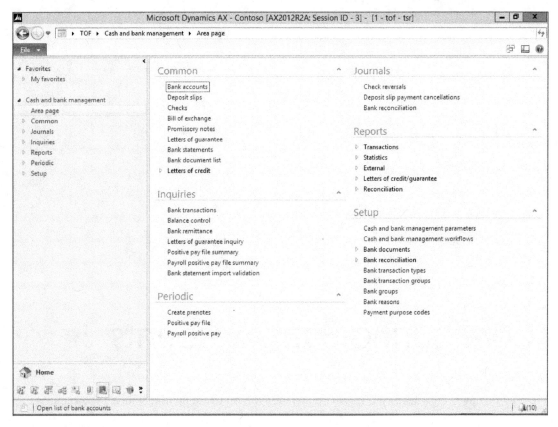

To do this, click on the **Bank Accounts** menu item within the **Common** group of the **Cash And Bank Management** area page.

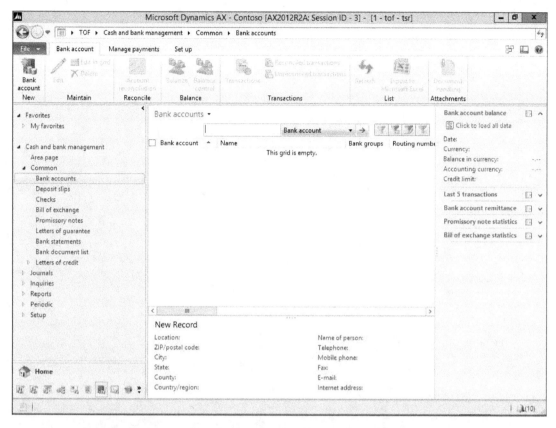

When the **Bank Accounts** list page is displayed, click on the **Bank Account** button within the **New** group of the **Bank Account** ribbon bar to create a new record.

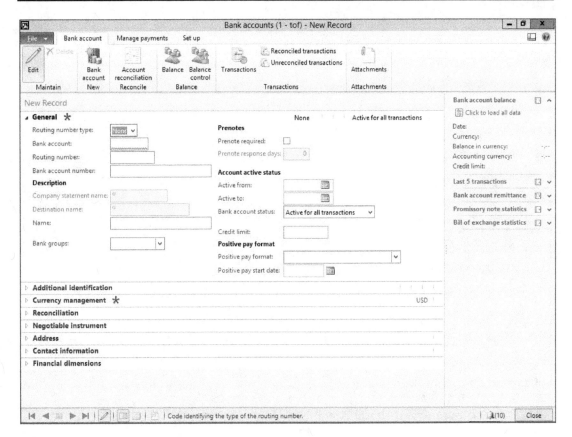

This will open up a new **Bank Account** record for you.

Give the record a **Bank Account** code of **OPER USD**.

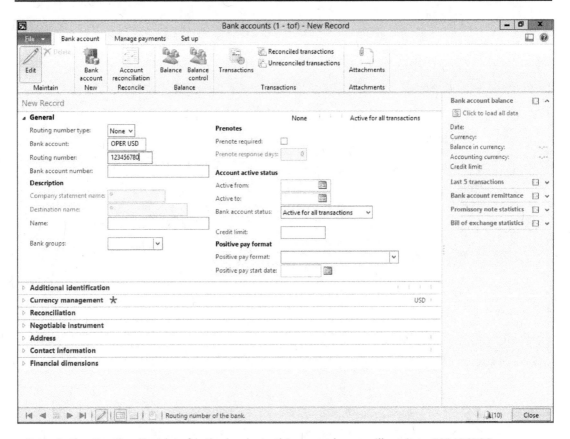

Enter in the **Routing Number** for the bank. In this example we will set it to **123456780**.

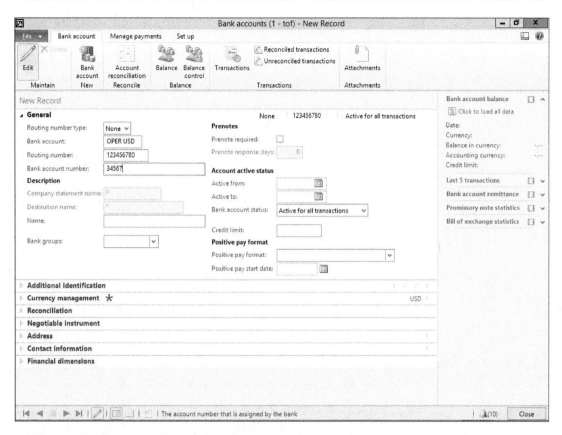

Then enter in the **Bank Account Number**. Use **34567** for this account.

And then give your **Bank Account** a descriptive **Name**. For this record set it to **Operating Bank Account – USD**.

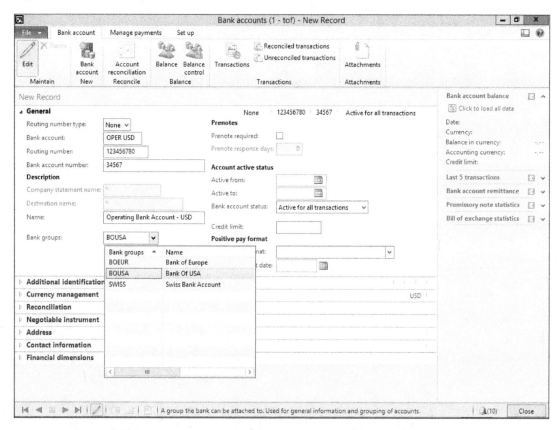

If your configured **Bank Groups** then you can select the group that you want to assign this **Bank Account** to. Select the **BOUSA** group for our US bank accounts

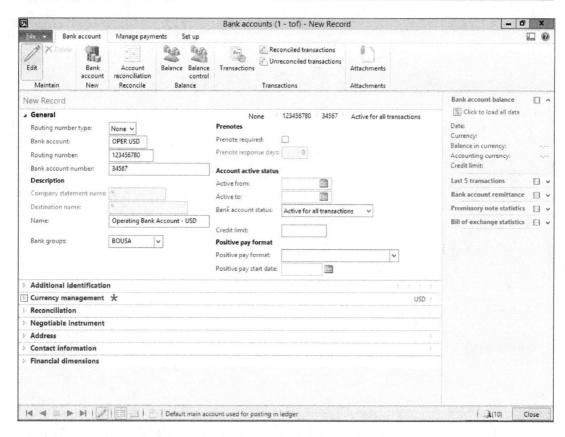

And that completes all of the general information for the **Bank Account**.

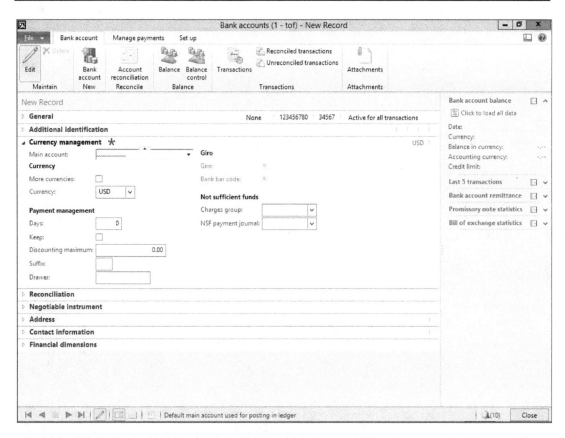

There is still a little more to do though. Open up the **Currency Management** tab and you will see that there is a little more information that is required.

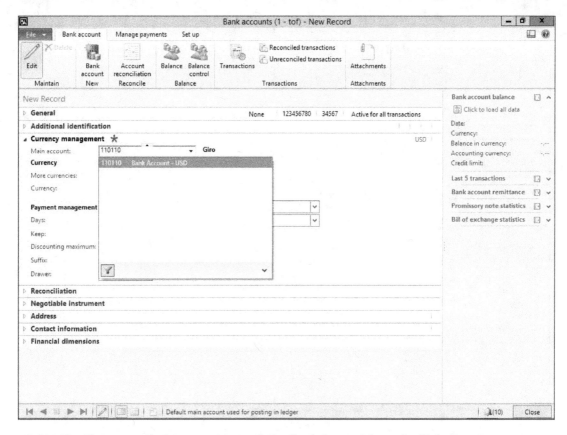

Select the GL account that you want to track the **Bank Account** from the **Main Account** dropdown. Use account number **110110** for this account.

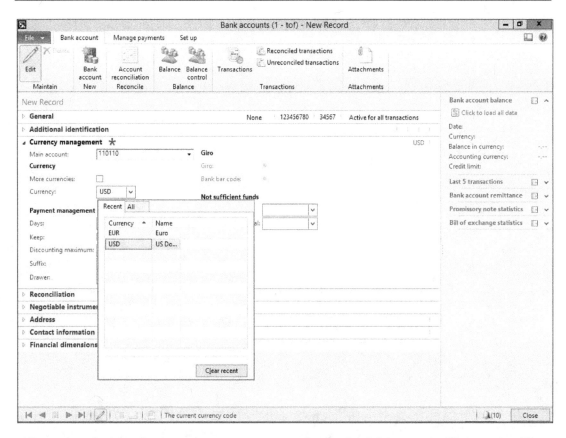

Then select the base **Currency** that you want to use for the **Bank Account**. In this case we will use **USD** as the base currency.

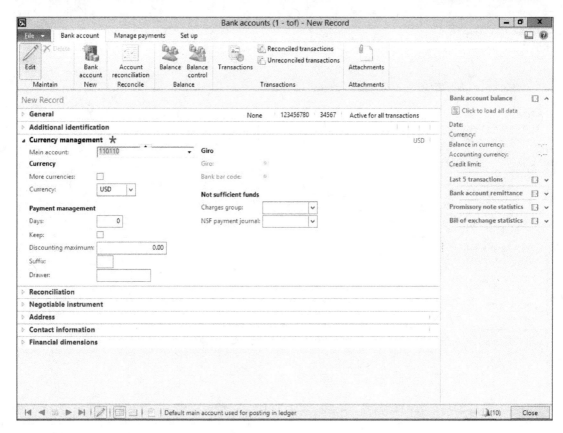

Now the first bank account is configured.

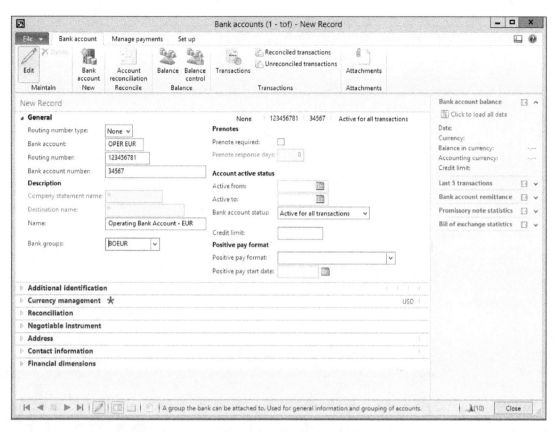

Click on the **New** button in the menu bar to create another bank account record. Set the **Bank Account** code to **OPER EUR**, the **Routing Number** to **123456781,** the **Bank Account Number** to **3456**, the **Name** to **Operating Account – EUR** and the **Bank Group** to **BOEUR**.

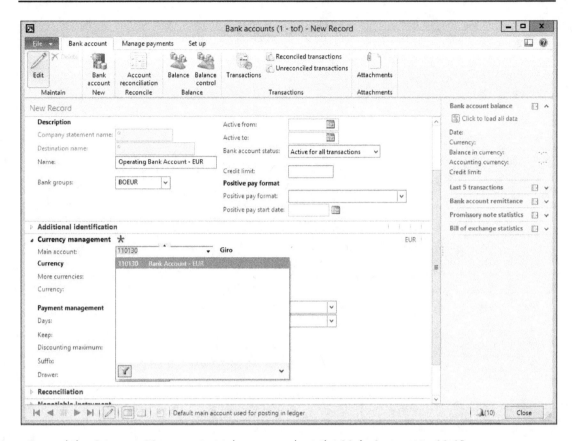

Expand the **Currency Management** tab group and set the **Main Account** to **11-13-**.

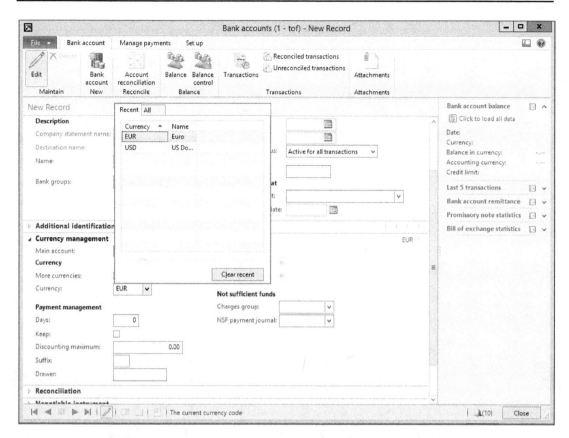

And then set the **Currency** to EUR.

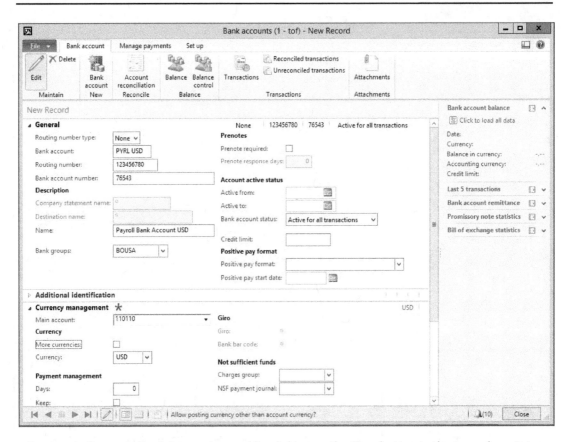

Create another new **Bank Account** record by clicking on the **New** button in the menu bar. Set the **Bank Account** code to PYRL USD, the **Routing Number** to 123456780, the **Bank Account Number** to 76543, the **Name** to Payroll Bank Account – USD, the **Bank Group** to BOUSA, the **Currency Management Main Account** to 110110, and the **Currency** to USD.

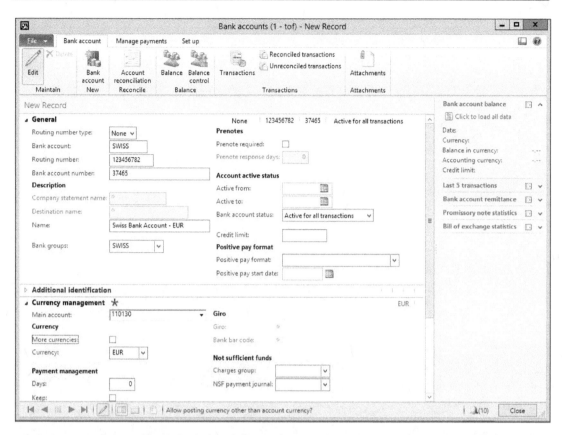

Finally create one last **Bank Account** record by clicking on the **New** button in the menu bar. Set the **Bank Account** code to SWISS, the **Routing Number** to 123456782, the **Bank Account Number** to 37465, the **Name** to Swiss Bank Account – EUR, the **Bank Group** to SWISS, the **Currency Management Main Account** to 110130, and the **Currency** to EUR.

If you want you can click the **Close** button and exit from the form.

Configuring Check Printing Formats

While you are configuring your **Bank Accounts** it may also be a good idea to quickly configure your check format.

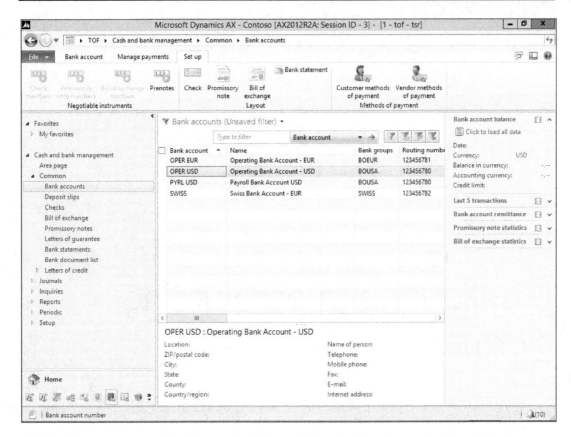

To do this, open up your **Bank Account** and then click on the **Check** menu button within the **Layouts** group of the **Setup** ribbon bar.

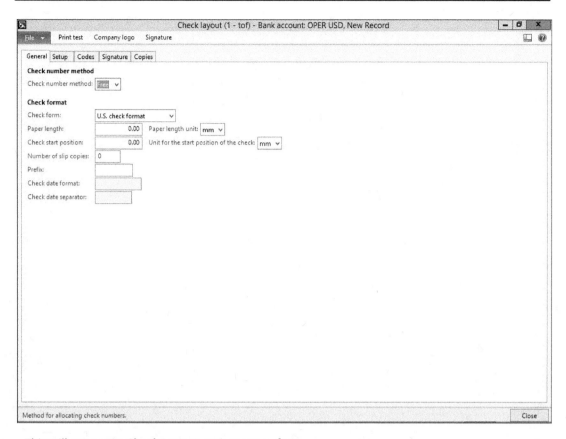

This will open up a **Check Layout** maintenance form.

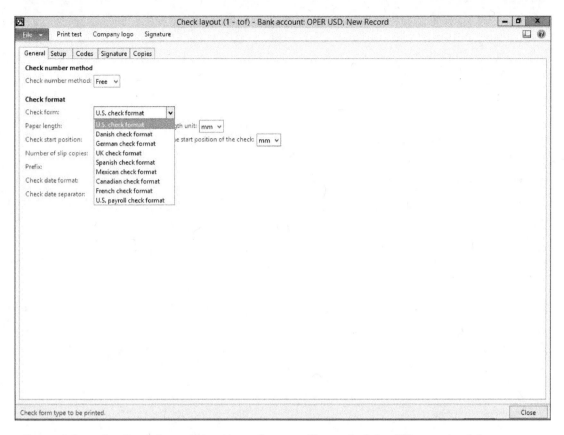

If you click on the **Check Format** dropdown list you will see all of the different check formats that are available to you. Select the US Check Format.

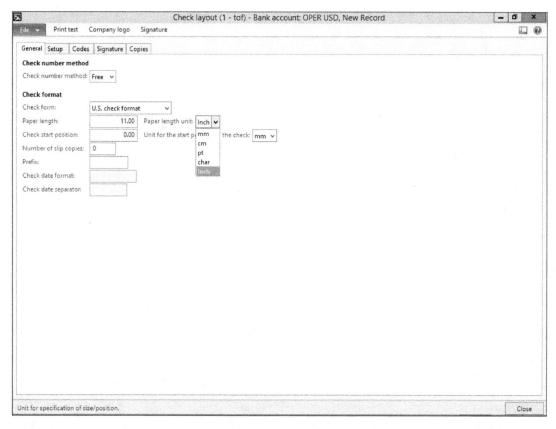

The first thing to do is to set the **Page Length** and the **Page Length Unit** – in this case 11 inches. Also you may want to change the default **Unit for start position of the check** to the same unit of measure.

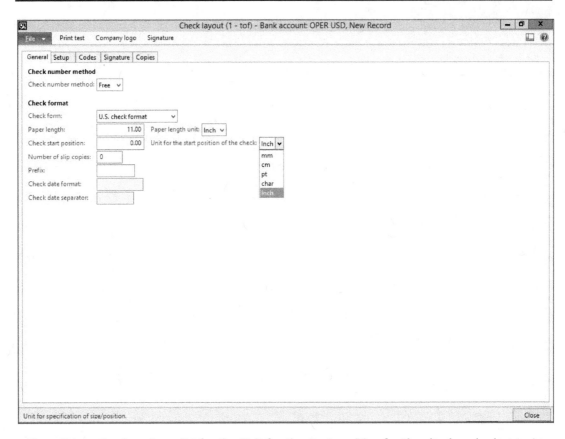

Also, click on the drop down list for the **Unit for the start position for the check** and select Inch.

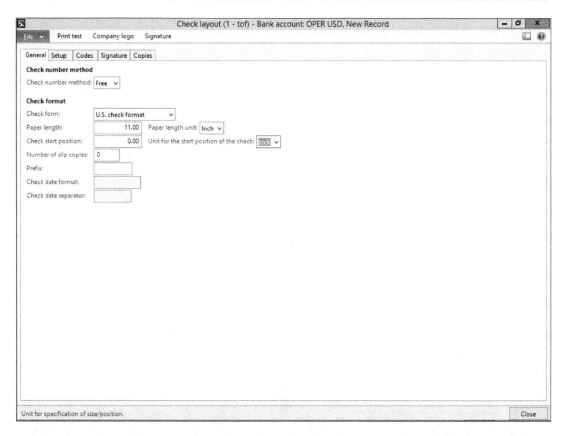

If you want to have a **Company Logo** show up on the check as well, click on the **Company Logo** menu item in the menu bar.

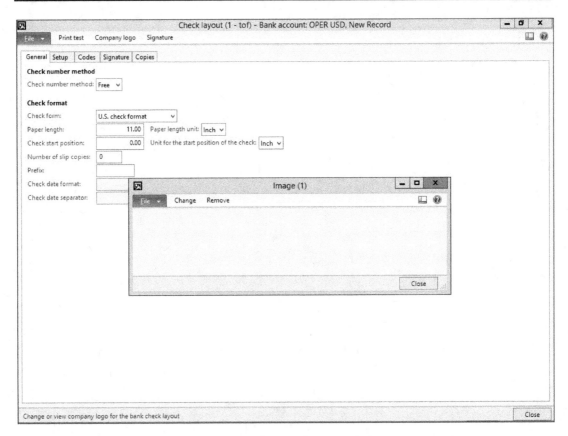

When the **Image** browser is displayed, click on the **Change** button in the menu bar.

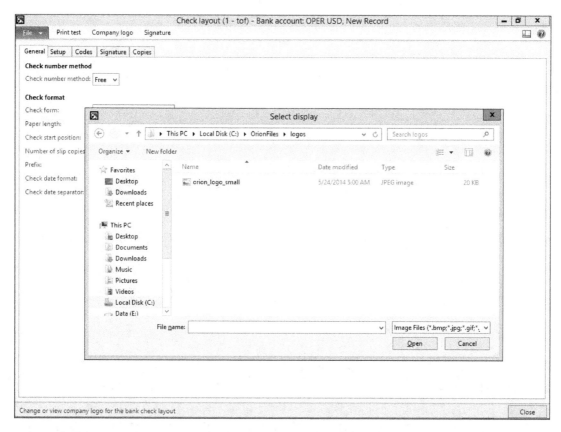

This will allow you to browse to the location where your default company logo is stored and **Open** it.

When you return to the **Image** dialog box you should be able to see the image and then click **Close** to exit from the form.

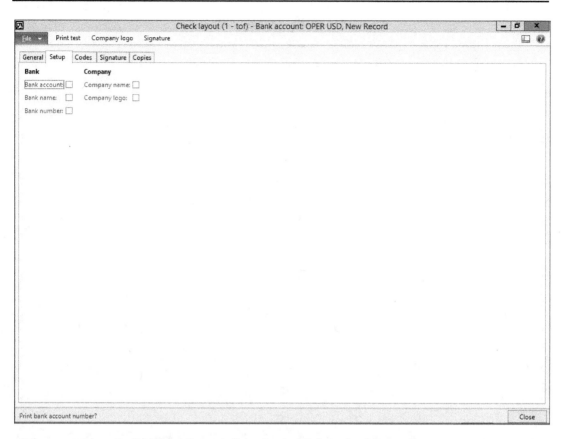

When you return to the **Check Layout** dialog box, switch to the **Setup** tab.

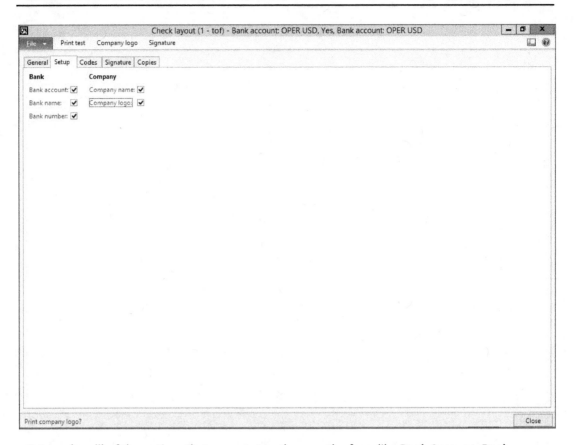

Set any (or all) of the options that you want to show on the form like **Bank Account**, **Bank Name**, **Bank Number**, **Company Name**, and /or **Company Logo.**

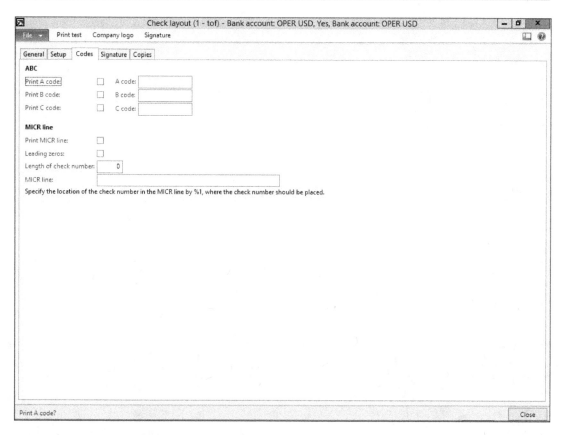

Then switch to the **Codes** tab.

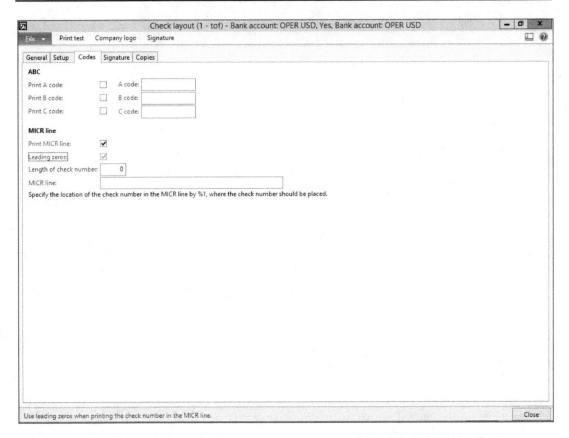

If you are using blank check stock, then you may want to check the **Print MICR Line** flag here.

Also you can check the **Leading Zeros** flag here as well to pad the values.

To test the check printing, just click on the **Print Test** item in the menu bar.

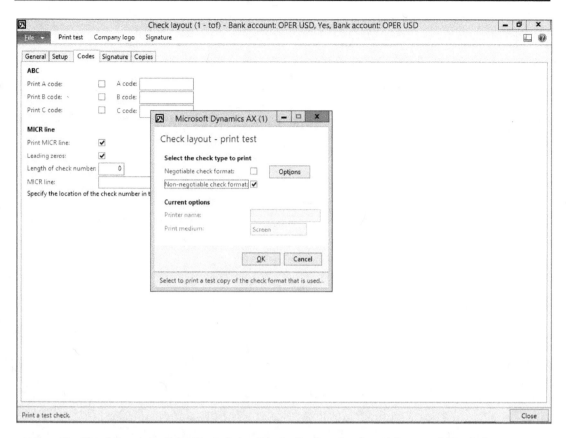

When the **Check Layout – Print Test** dialog box is displayed, select the type of check that you want to print, and then click the **OK** button.

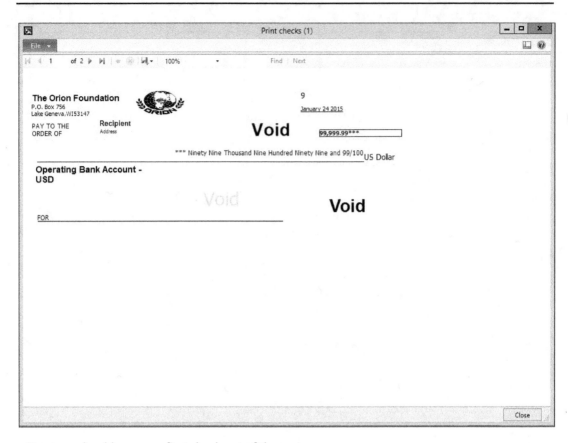

Now you should see your first check out of the system.

How easy is that?

Adding Signatures To Checks

If you want to have the signatures automatically printed on the checks then you can also do that within the check configuration form.

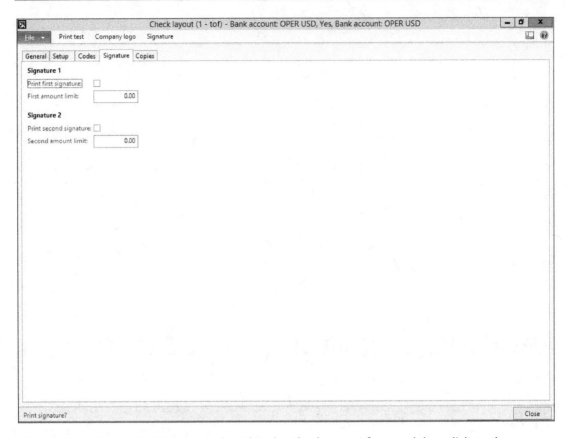

To do this switch to the **Signature** tab within the **Check Layout** form and then click on the **Signature** button within the menu bar.

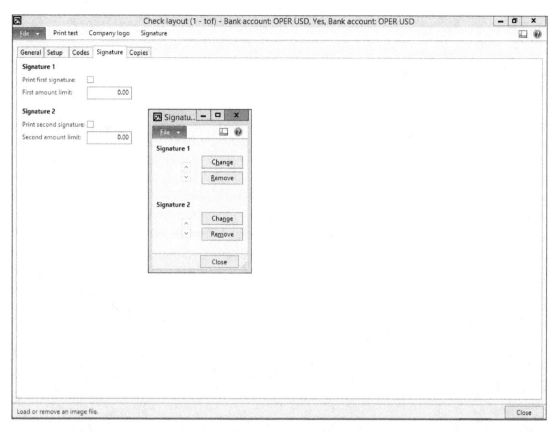

When the **Signatures** dialog box is displayed, click on the **Change** button for the first signature.

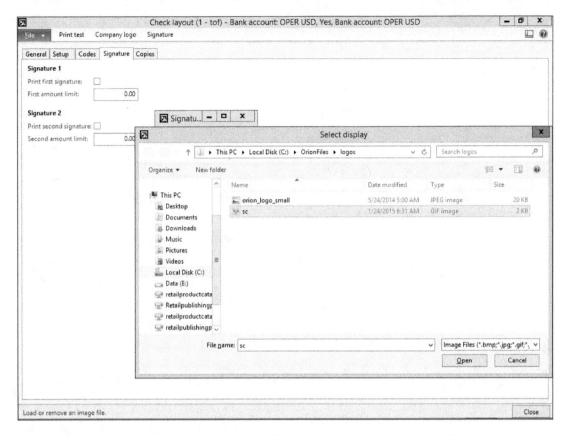

This will allow you to browse to the signature file that you want to use for the first signature block. Select the file and then click on the **Open** button.

When you return back to the **Signature** form you will see that the image has been loaded into the first **Signature** area. You can add a second signature if you like and then click on the **Close** button to exit from the form.

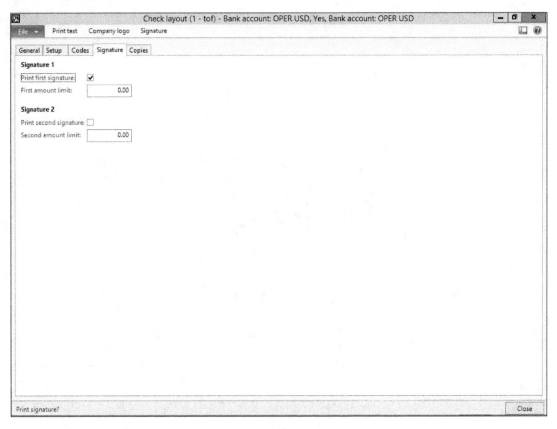

To use the signature, just check the **Print First Signature** check box.

When you are done you can exit from the form.

Assigning the Bank to The Organization

Once you have your **Bank Accounts** configured, there is just one loose end that you will probably want to tie up and that is to link the **Bank Account** to your **Organization**.

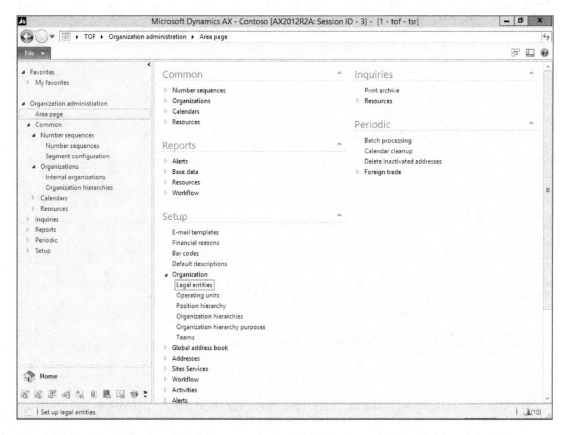

To do this, click on the **Legal Entities** menu item within the **Organizations** folder of the **Setup** group within the **Organization Administration** area page.

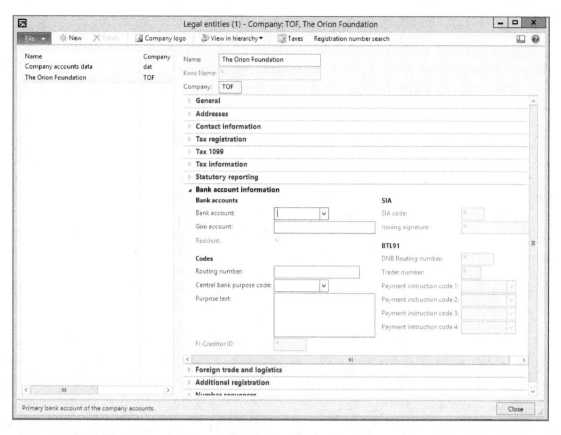

When the **Legal Entities** maintenance form is displayed, select your main **Legal Entity** and then open up the **Bank Account Information** tab.

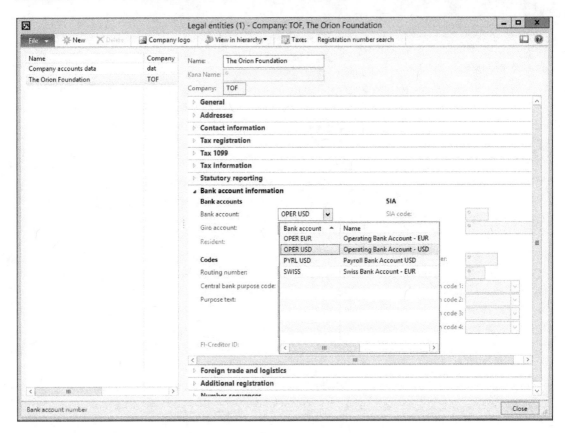

You will now be able to select your default **Bank Account** from the dropdwn list.

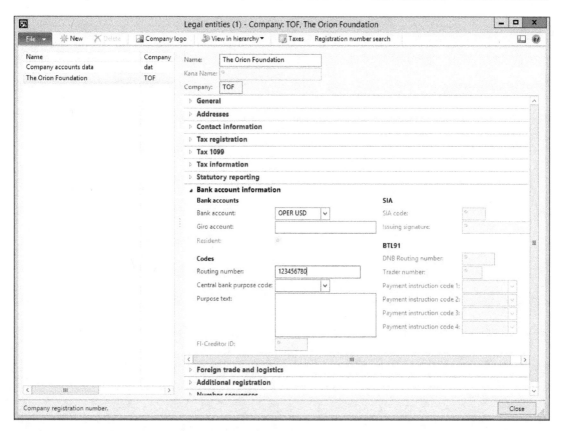

After you have entered in the **Routing Number** for the bank account, you can click on the **Close** button and exit from the form.

Reconciling Bank Accounts

Now that you have the bank accounts configured you can start using them. The first thing that you may want to do is reconcile them. In this section we will show you the simple bank reconciliation option.

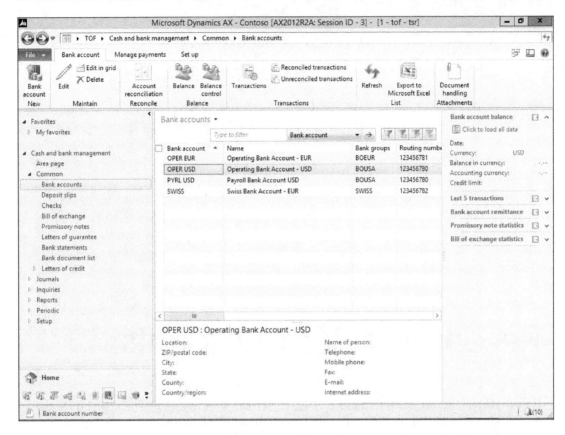

To do this, open up your **Bank Account** and then click on the **Account Reconciliation** menu button within the **Reconcile** group of the **Bank Account** ribbon bar.

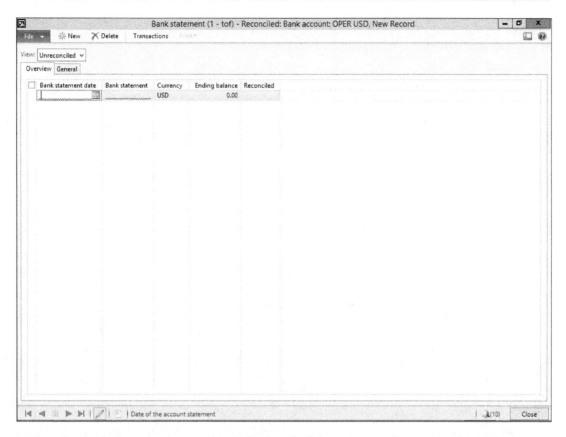

When the **Bank Statement** menu item is displayed, click on the **New** button to create a new record.

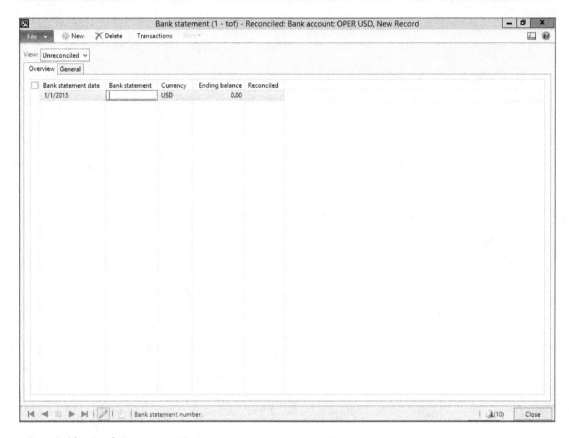

Type in the **Bank Statement Date**.

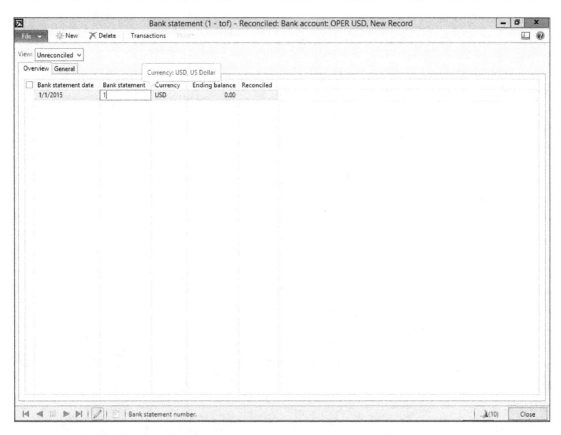

Then enter in the **Bank Statement** number.

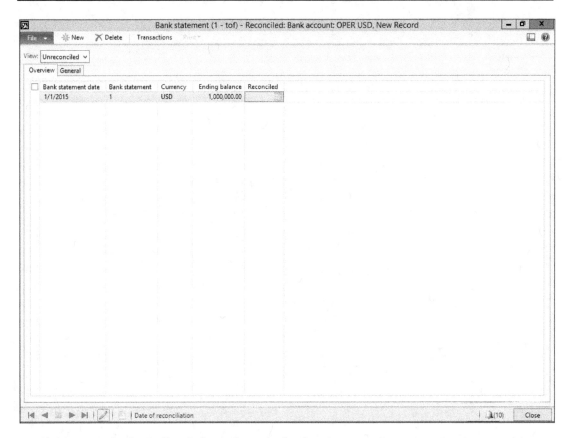

And then enter in the **Ending Balance** from the bank statement. Once you save the record (**CTRL+S**) you will then be able to click on the **Transactions** button within the menu bar to start entering in the bank statement transactions.

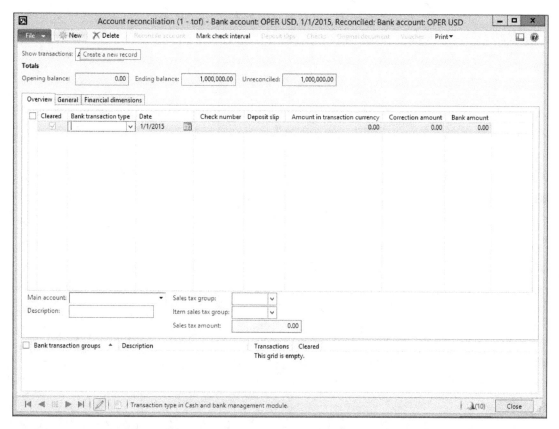

When the **Account Reconciliation** maintenance form is displayed, click on the **New** button in the menu bar to create a new line.

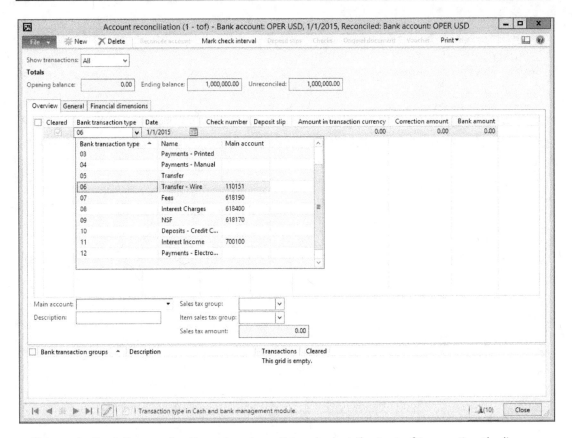

Click on the **Bank Transaction Type** dropdown list and select the type of transaction the line refers to. In this case we will use **06** for a **Wire Transfer**.

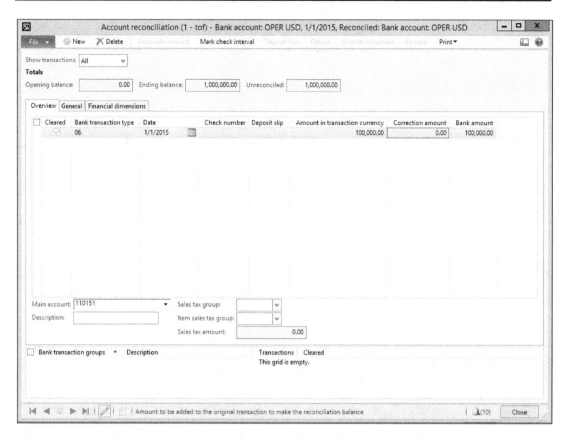

Then enter in the line amount into the **Amount in Transaction Currency** field.

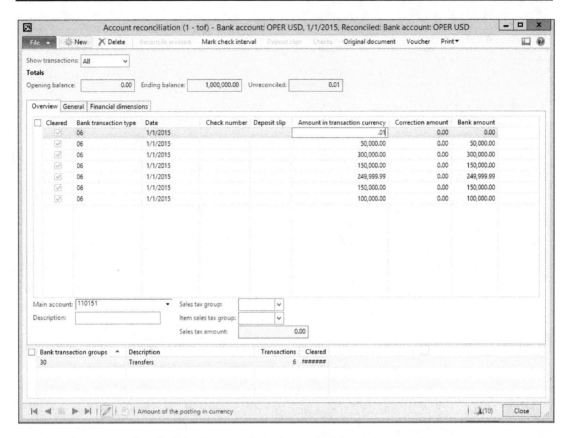

Repeat the process for all of the lines until you have all of the statement lines.

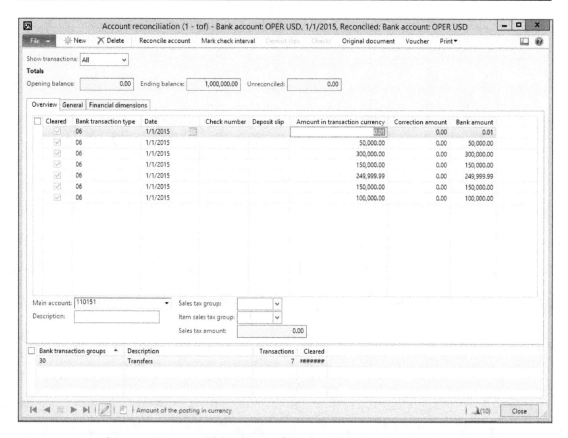

As soon as you have an **Unreconciled Balance** of 0, you will notice that the **Reconcile Account** button in the menu bar becomes enabled, and you are able to click on it.

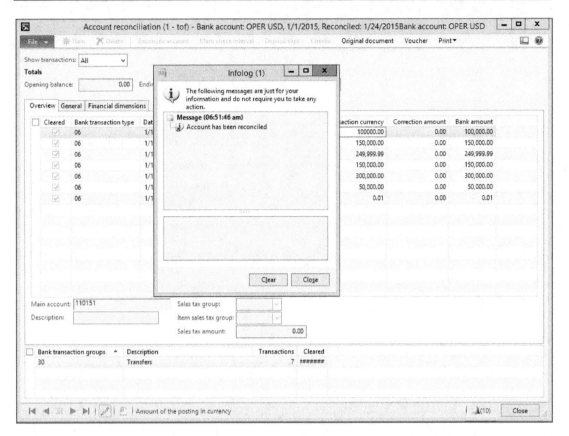

You will then get an InfoLog that tells you that the account has been reconciled and you can exit from the form.

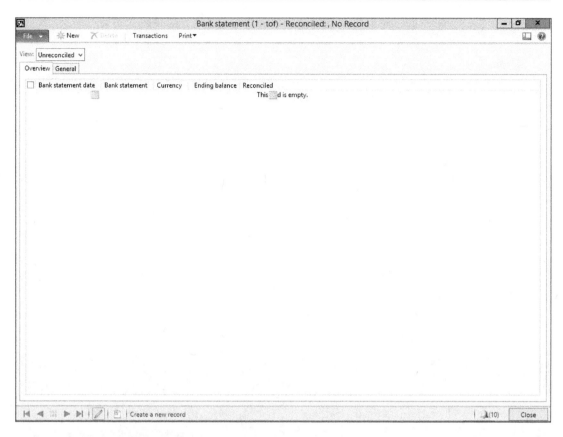

When you return back to the **Bank Statement** list you will see that the record that you have just entered is no longer showing.

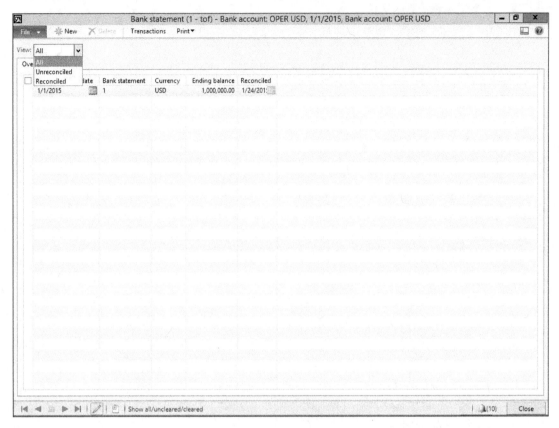

If you click on the **View** button and change the option to **All** then you will see the posted transaction.

Now you can click on the **Close** button to exit from the form.

Viewing Bank Account Statistics

If you want to see the effects of the Bank Statement Reconciliation then you can easily see the transactions and the bank statistics within the **Bank Account** record itself.

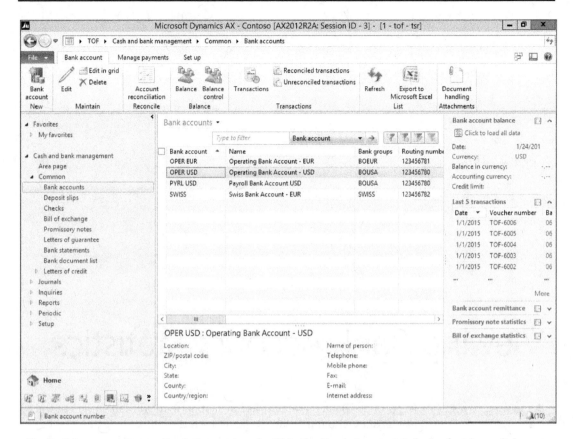

To do this, open up your **Bank Account** and within the **Bank Account Balance** fact box, click on the **Click To Load All Data** link.

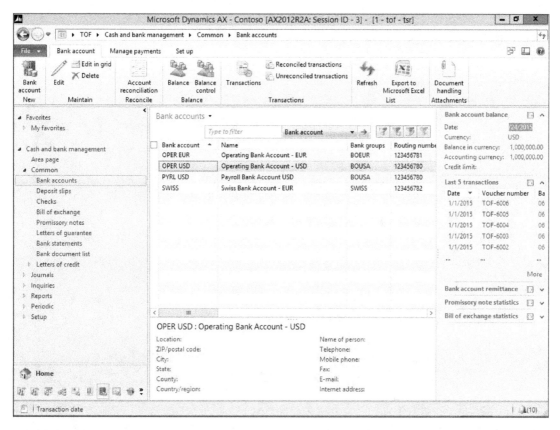

That will load in the bank account statistics and you will see the account balance and the balance date.

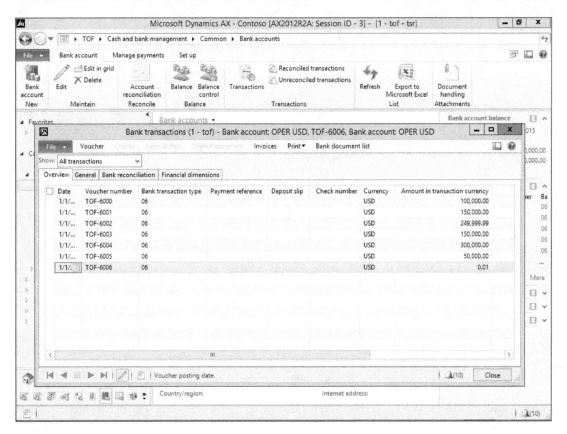

If you want to see all of the posted transactions then you can also click on the **Transactions** button within the **Transactions** group of the **Bank Account** ribbon bar. That will open up a list page showing you all of the transactions that have been posted to the bank account.

CONFIGURING ADVANCED BANK RECONCILIATION

The Advanced Bank Reconciliation feature within Dynamics AX is a great function to enable because it automates so much of the bank statement administration and also gives to better bank reconciliation matching functions that will save you hours of manual work. The first feature that you will want to look into though is the ability to import all of your bank statements directly from the bank file.

This may seem like a daunting task because it seems as though there is a lot of technical configuration to perform in order to get the system to read the file, but it's not really the case. In this walkthrough we will show you how you can easily configure the **Advanced Bank Reconciliation** statement import feature.

That will give you more time to spend with your money.

Configuring A Reconciliation Approval Workflow

Before we start setting up the **Advanced Bank Reconciliation** though we will take a little time to set up a workflow that we will use to streamline the approval of the Reconciled accounts. This will allow us to add a little control over the reconciliation process.

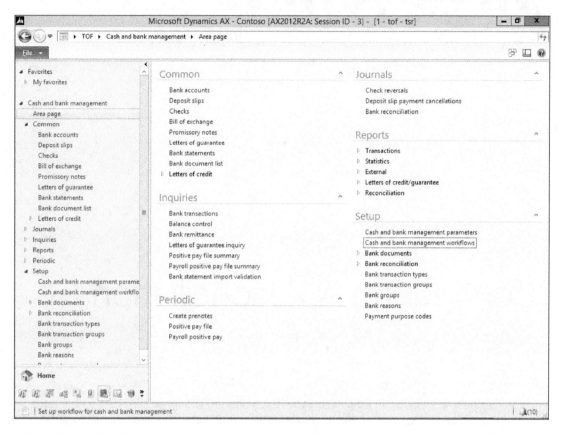

To do this, click on the **Cash and Bank Management Workflows** menu item within the **Setup** group of the **Cash and Bank Management** area page.

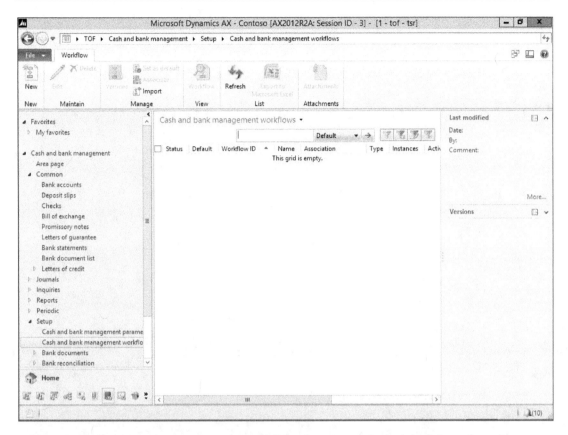

When the **Cash and Bank Management Workflows** list page is displayed, click on the **New** button within the **New** group of the **Workflow** ribbon bar.

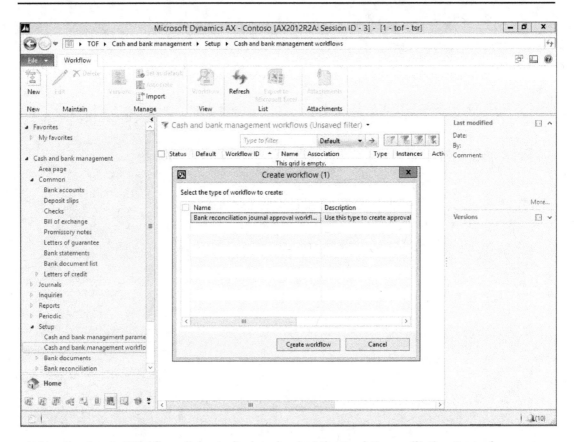

When the **Create Workflow** dialog is displayed, select the **Bank Reconciliation Journal Approval Workflow** template and then click on the **Create Workflow** button.

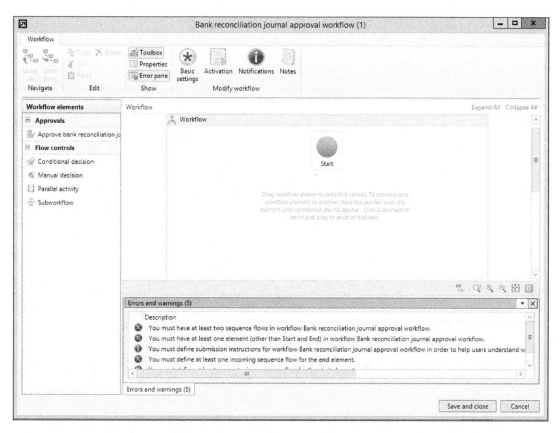

This will open up the workflow designer.

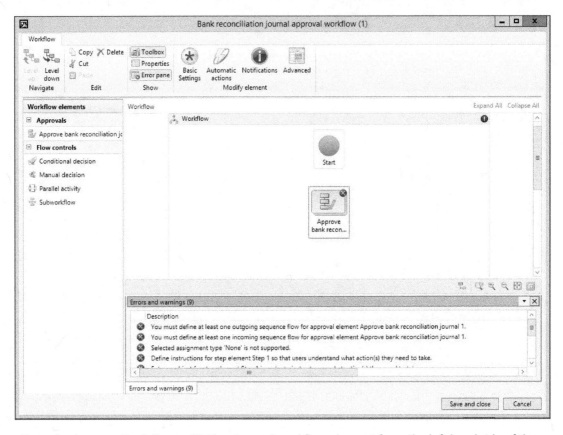

Drag the **Approve Bank Reconciliation Journal** workflow element from the left hand side of the designer onto the workflow canvas.

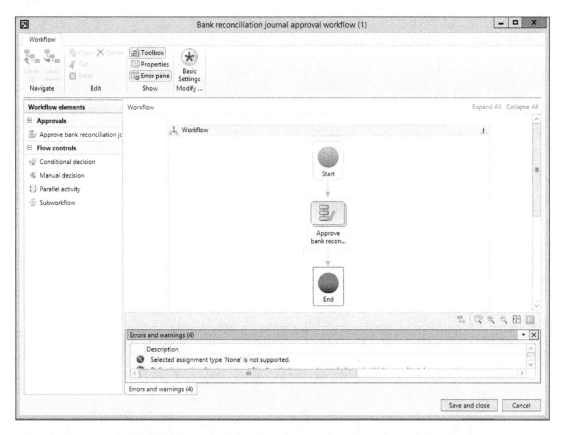

Now hover over the **Start** node and when the connector icons are shown, drag the mouse down to the **Approve Bank Reconciliation Journal** element to connect them.

Do the same again to connect the **Approve Bank Reconciliation Journal** element and the **End** node to create a linked workflow.

You will notice that there are a number of Errors and Warning displayed at the bottom of the form that shows you a number of loose ends that need to be tied up. Click on the first one.

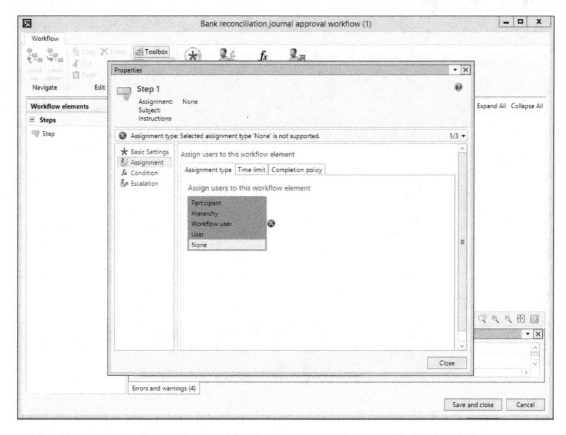

This will open up the **Properties** panel for the **Approve Bank Reconciliation Journal** step where we need to assign someone to the workflow step.

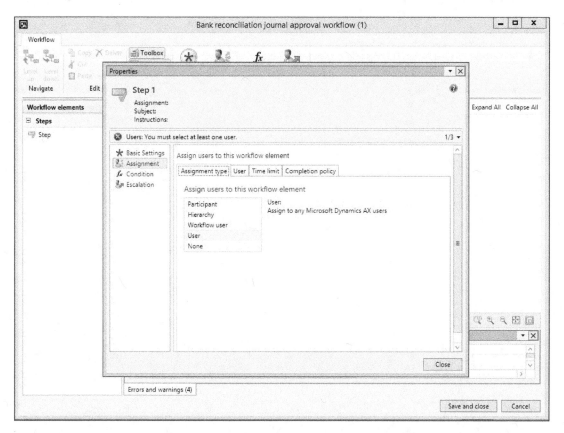

Within the **Assign Users To This Workflow** option list, select the **User** option.

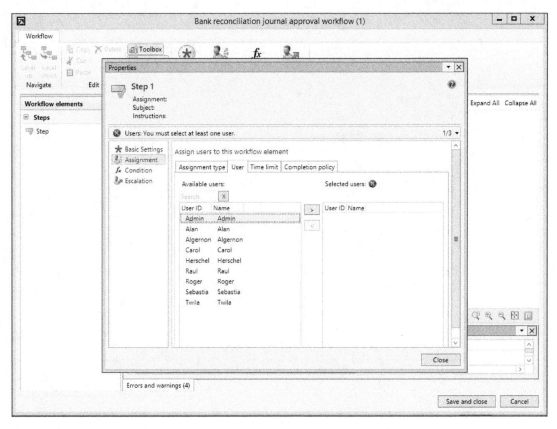

Then switch to the **User** tab and you will see all of the users that we can include in this workflow.

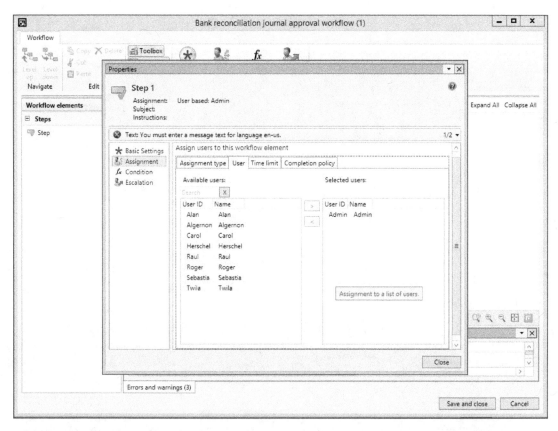

Select the **Admin** user and then click on the **>** button to add the user to the **Selected Users**.

When you have done that click on the **Close** button to exit from the form.

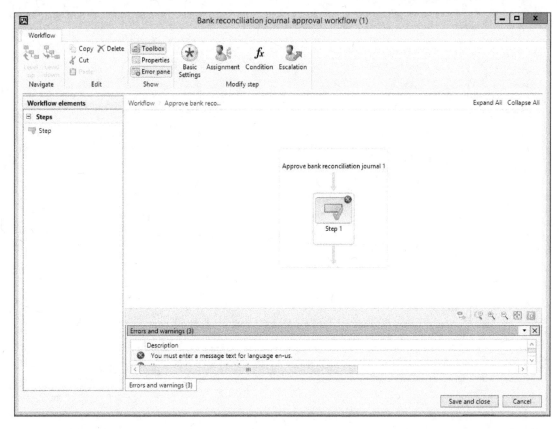

When you return to the **Bank Reconciliation Journal Approval Workflow** you will see that the error message is gone, but there are still some things that you need to fix. So click on the next error in the list.

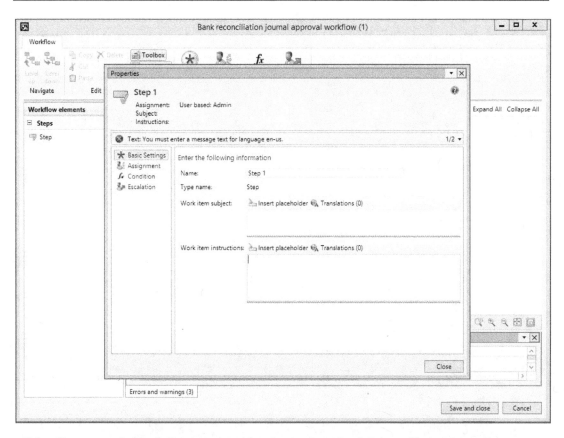

This will open up the **Basic Settings** panel for the **Approve Bank Reconciliation Journal** step where we need to add some explanations and messages to the workflow step.

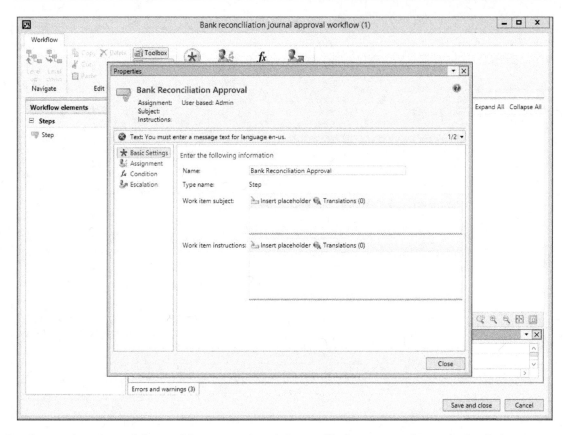

Change the **Name** of the workflow step to **Bank Reconciliation Approval** to make it a little clearer as to the purpose of the step.

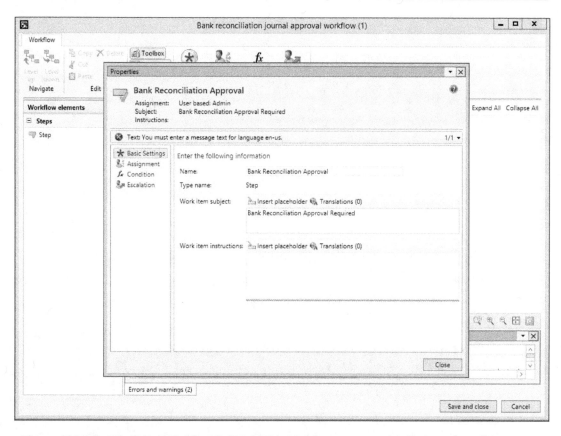

Then within the **Work Item Subject** field add the text that you want to display when the workflow task is assigned to the user. A good example of this would be Bank Reconciliation Approval Required.

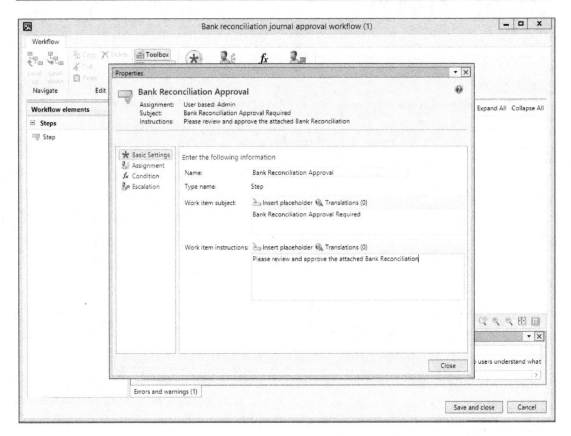

Then within the **Work Item Instructions** type in a brief description of what you want the approver to do. For example you may use Please review and approve the attached Bank Reconciliation.

After you have done that click on the **Close** button to exit from the form.

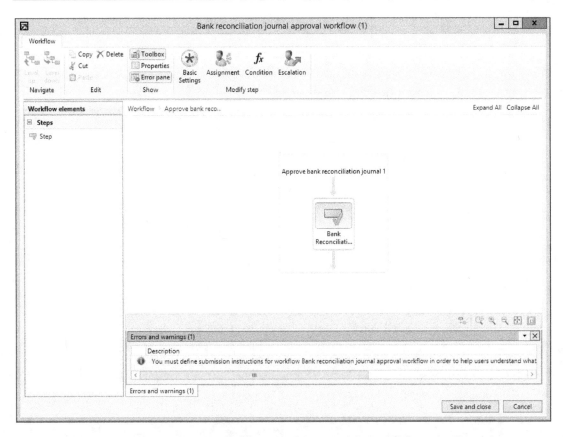

When you return to the **Bank Reconciliation Journal Approval Workflow** you will see that there is one last item that needs to be fixed so double click on it.

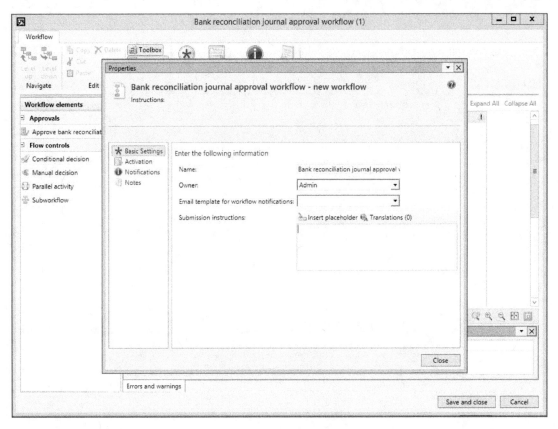

This will open up the **Basic Settings** panel for the whole workflow where we need to add some submission instructions.

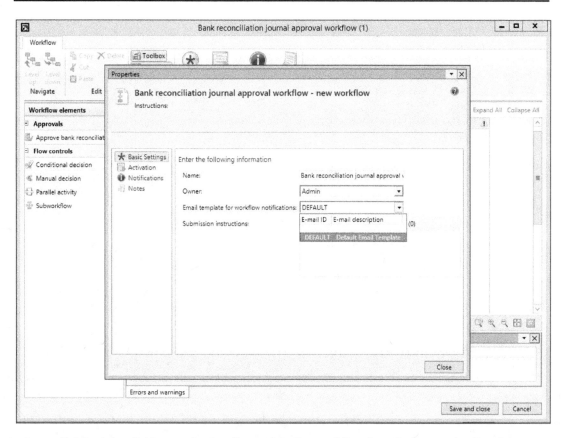

Start off though by clicking on the **Email template for workflow instructions** and select the
DEFAULT email template.

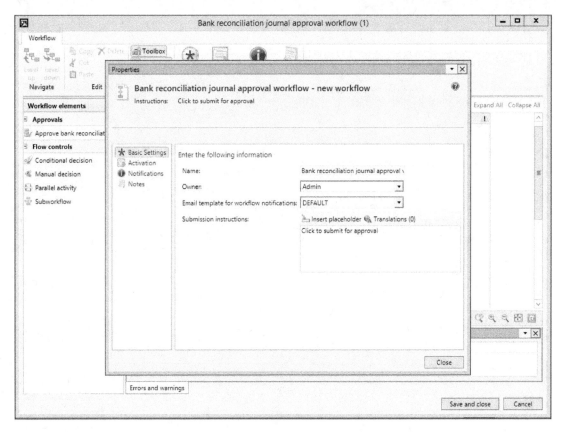

Then enter in some **Submission Instructions** for the user to see when they are asked to submit the reconciliation for approval. For example you could type Click to submit for approval.
When you are done, click on the **Close** button to exit from the form.

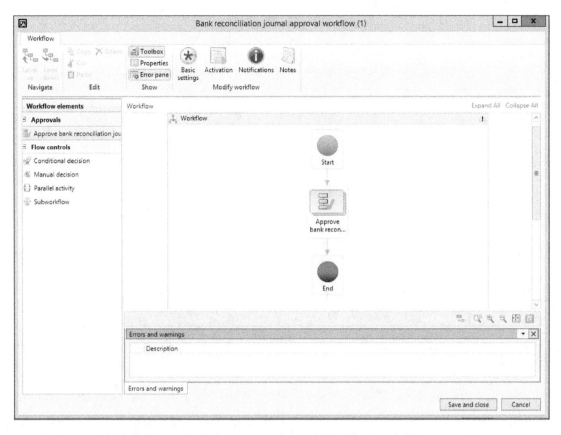

Returning to the **Bank Reconciliation Journal Approval Workflow** you will see that there are no more errors or warnings and you can click on the **Save And Close** button.

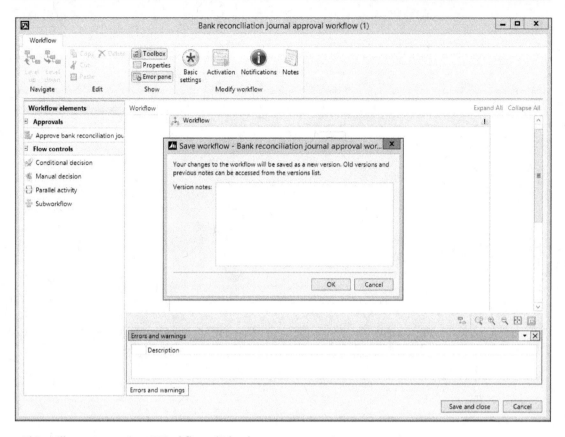

This will open up a **Save Workflow** dialog box.

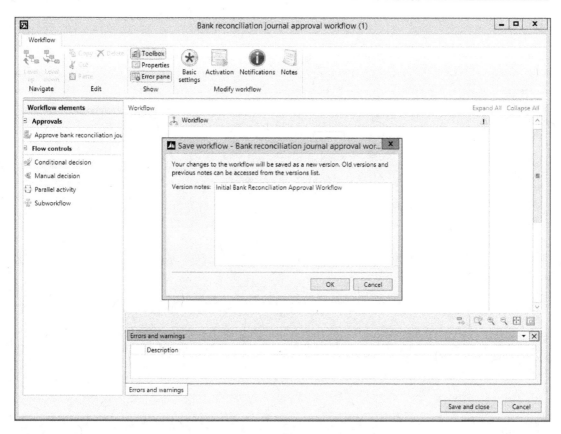

You can type in a description of the workflow within the **Version Notes** field and then click on the **OK** button.

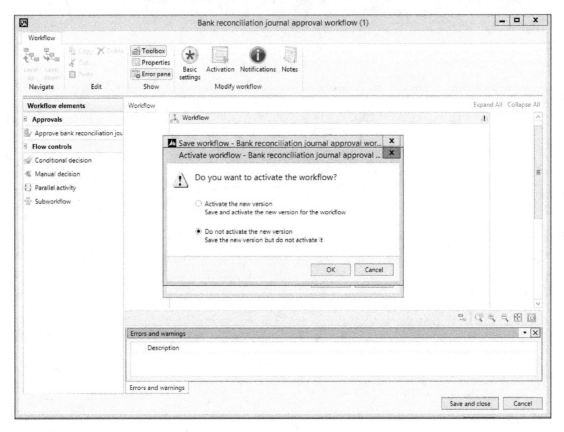

Then an **Activate Workflow** dialog box will be shown asking you if you want to leave your workflow in the inactive state or start using it.

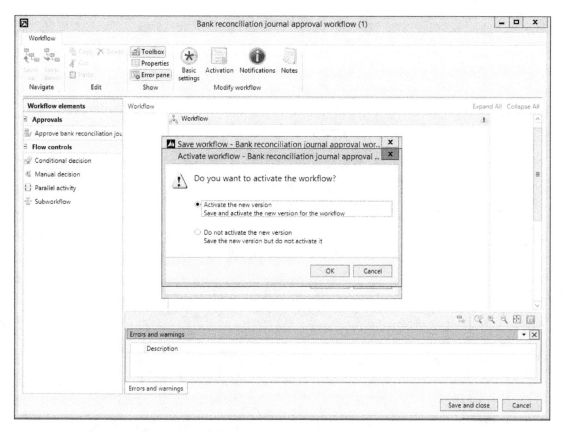

Click on the **Activate the New Version** option and then click on the **OK** button.

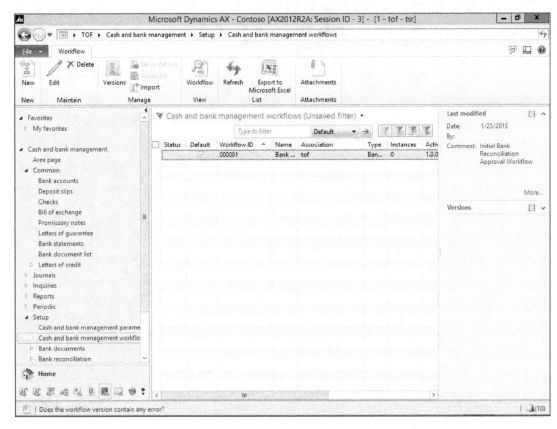

When you return to the **Cash and Bank Management** workflows list you will see that you have a new workflow.

Getting The Transformation Style Sheet Resources

Since the most common way that the bank reconciliation files com to you as a text file, we need to have a way to massage the file into a format that Dynamics AX is able to use for the import. The way that this is done is through XML style sheet transformations (XSLT). Don't worry though – you don't have to hand craft this file – it's already saved away for you within the AOT for you to download and start using.

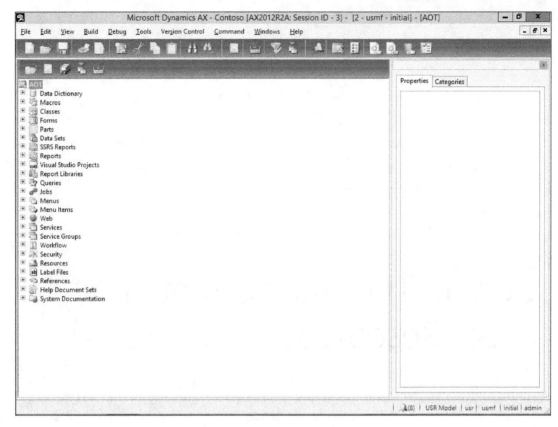

To do this start off by opening up AOT.

Tip: If you are in AX and have developer rights then just press **CTRL+D**.

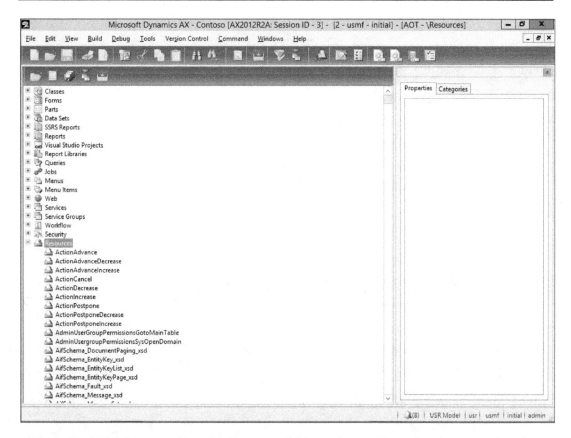

Within the AOT tree, expand out the **Resources** folder and you will see that there are a lot of goodies files away there for you to use.

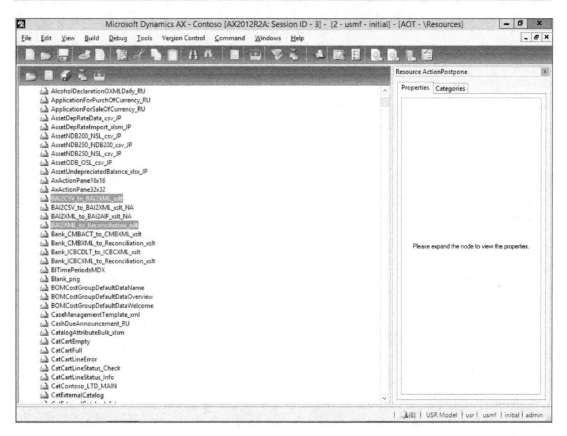

Scroll down the list and you will see that there are a number of different bank transformation files that are available for you to use. The ones that we are interested are for the BAI2 format, and are the **BAI2CSV_to_BAI2XML_xslt** file which will convert the CSV file into an XML file, and also the **BAI2XML_to_Reconciliation_xslt** file that converts the XML file into something that AIF is able to read.

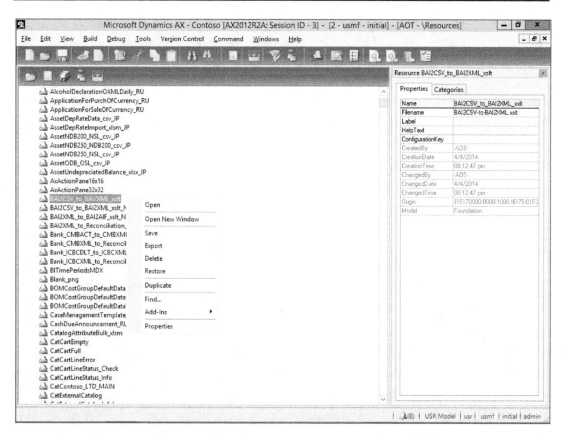

Right-mouse-click on the **BAI2CSV_to_BAI2XML_xslt** file and select the **Open** option.

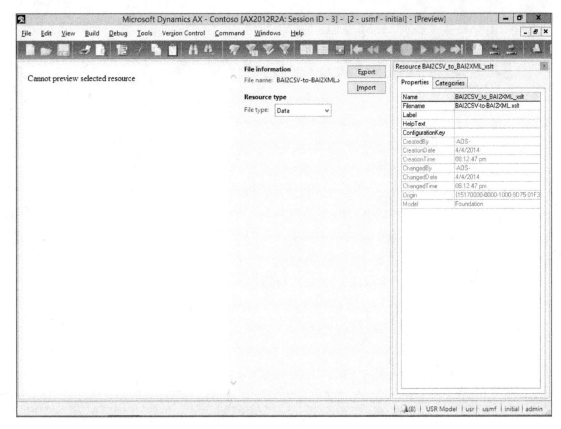

This will open up a new resource window for the file.

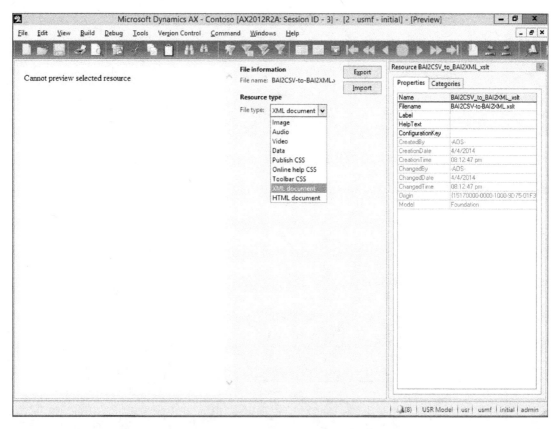

Click on the **File Type** dropdown list and change it to **XML document**.

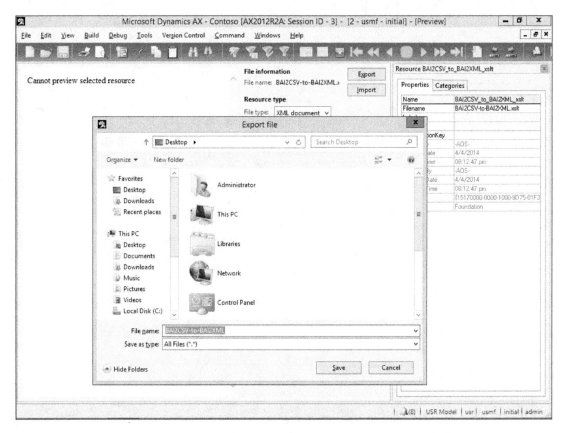

And then click on the **Export** button and save the file to your desktop.

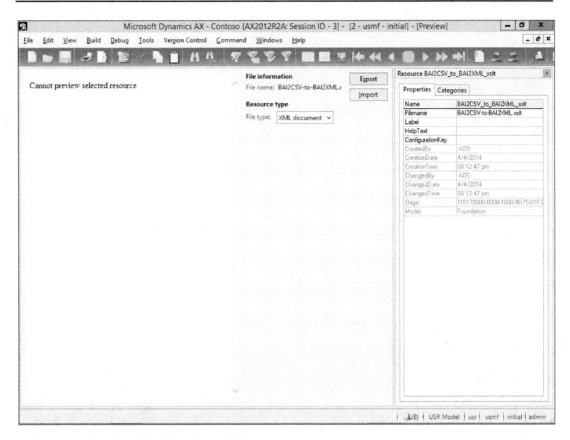

After you are done, just close the window.

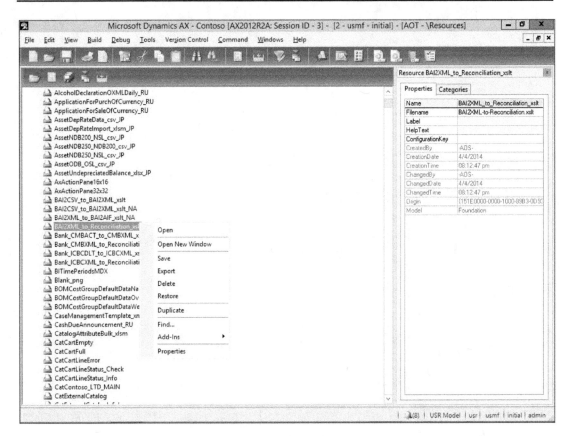

Next right-mouse-click on the **BAI2XML_to_Reconciliation_xslt** file and click on the **Open** menu item.

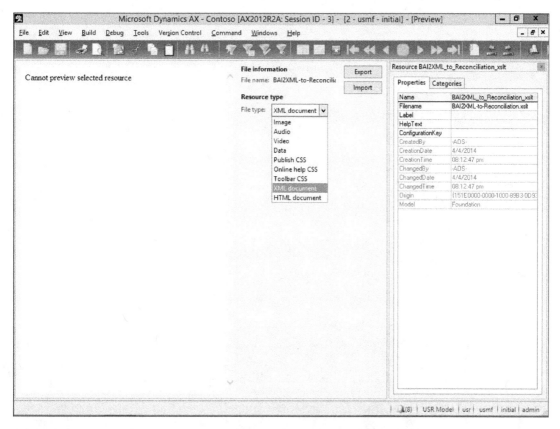

When the resource form is displayed, click on the **File Type** dropdown list and change it to **XML document**.

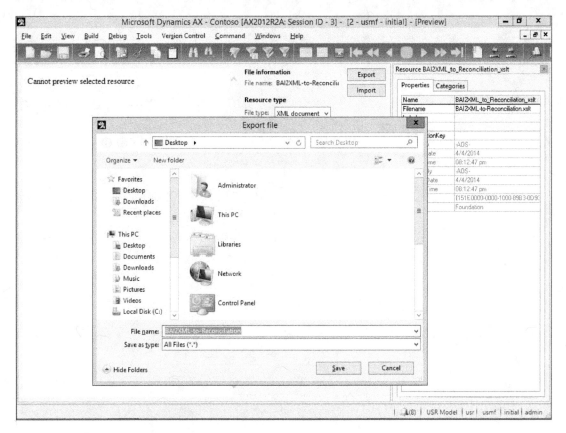

And then click on the **Export** button and save the file to your desktop.

After you are done, just close the window.

Creating The Transformation Rules

Now that we have the transformation files, we want to create a rule that will use the files to convert the CSV files into a format for the reconciliation to use.

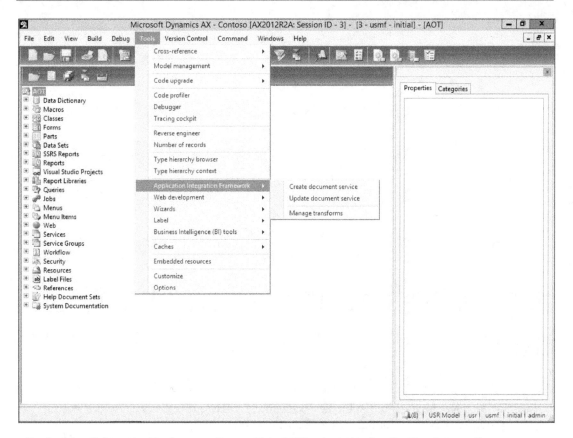

To do this, click on the **Tools** menu item within **AOT**, select the **Application Integration Framework** menu item and select the **Manage Transforms** menu item.

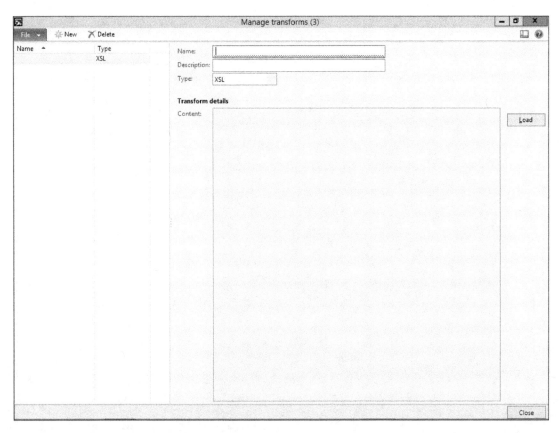

When the **Manage Transforms** maintenance form is displayed, click on the **New** button in the menu bar to create a new record.

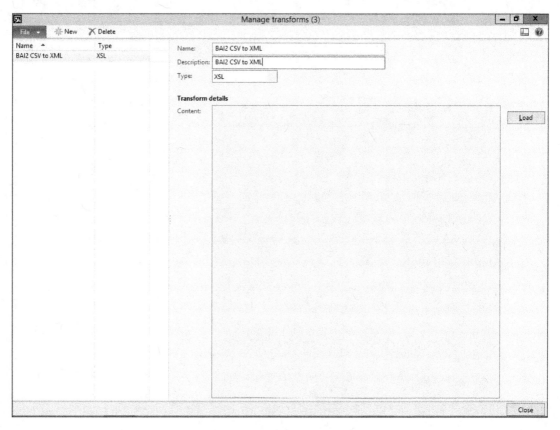

Give the new record a **Name** and **Description** of **BAI2 CSV to XML**.

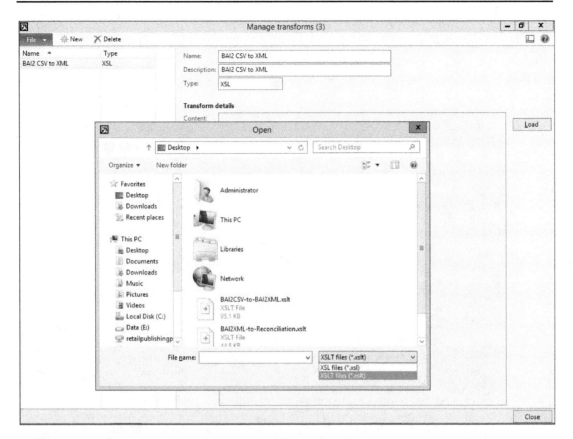

Then click on the **Load** button to import in the XSLT file that you just downloaded from the Resources.

Tip: You may need to change the file type to **XSLT files** in order to see them though.

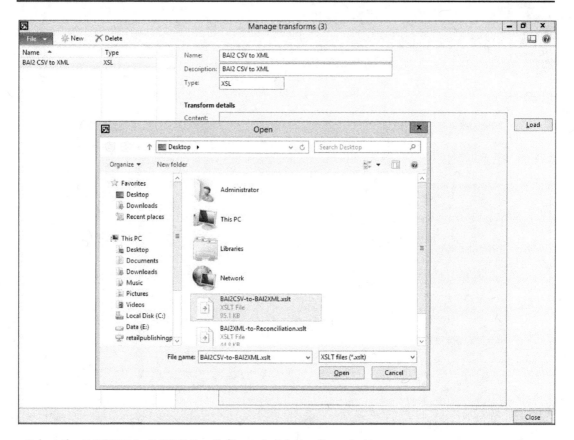

Select the **BAI2CSV-to-BAI2XML.xslt** file and click the **Open** button.

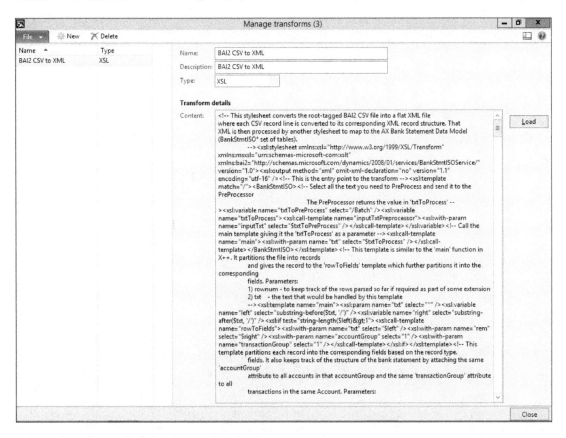

Now you will see all of the XSLT within the **Content** section.

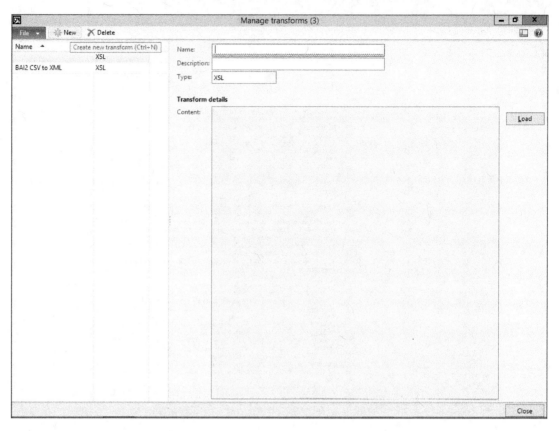

Click on the **New** button in the menu bar to create another record.

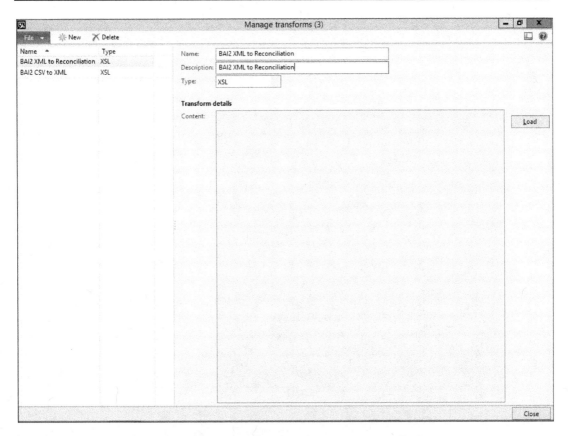

Give the new record a **Name** and **Description** of **BAI2 XML to Reconciliation**.

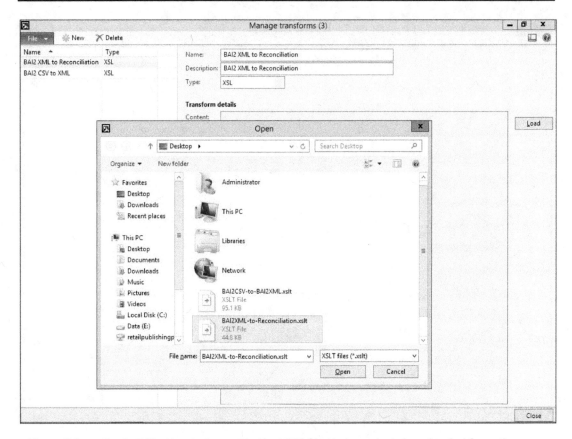

Then click on the **Load** button to import in the XSLT file that you just downloaded from the Resources and this time select the **BAI2XML-to-Reconciliation.xslt**

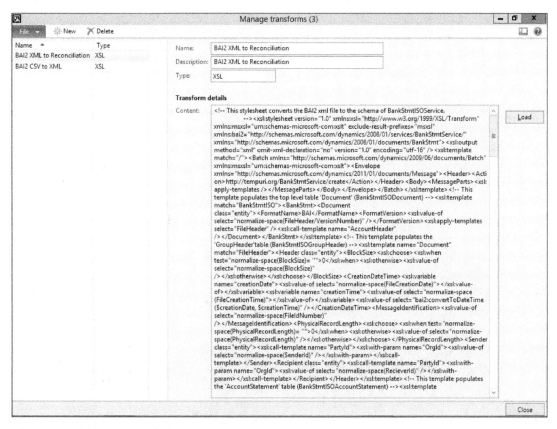

Once you have done that you can exit from the form.

Configuring The AIF Port To Process The Inbound Files

The importing of the Bank Reconciliation file is actually being done through AIF and the AIF ports and we need to configure one that will be used to turn our CSV files into Bank Statements within Dynamics AX. For the non-developer these may seem a little daunting to configure, but it's not really that hard.

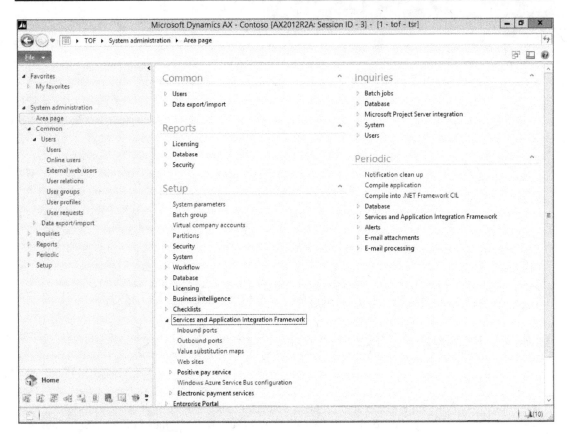

To do this, click on the **Inbound Ports** menu item within the **Services and Application Integration Framework** folder of the **Setup** group within the **System Administration** area page.

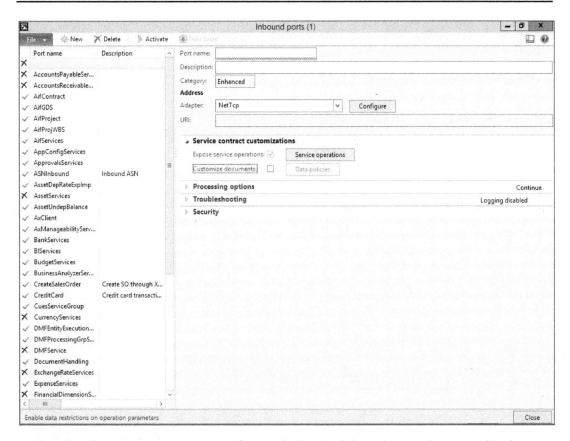

When the **Inbound Ports** maintenance form is displayed, click on the **New** button within the menu bar to create a new record.

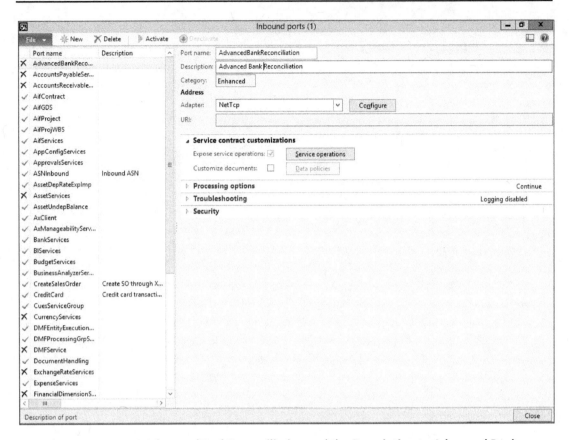

Set the **Port Name** to **AdvancedBankReconciliation** and the **Description** to **Advanced Bank Reconciliation.**

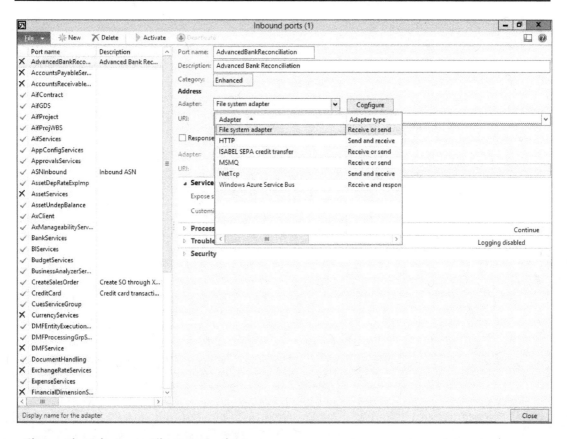

Change the **Adapter** to **File system adapter**.

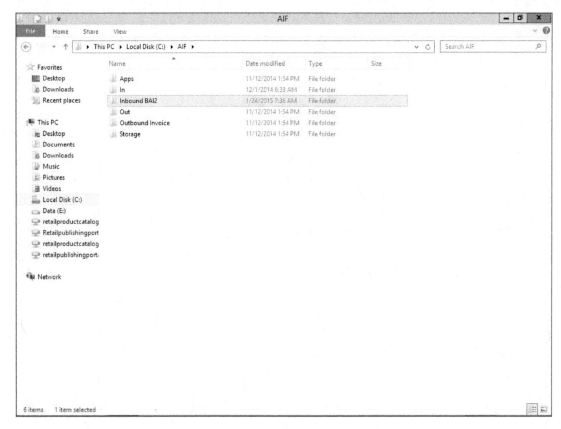

Now create a folder that you will put all of your bank statement files into.

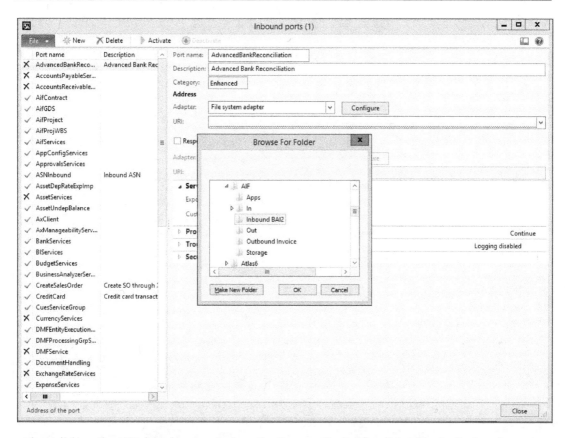

Then click on the **URI** dropdown and when the **Browse For Folder** dialog box is displayed, navigate to the inbound file folder that you just created and click on the **OK** button.

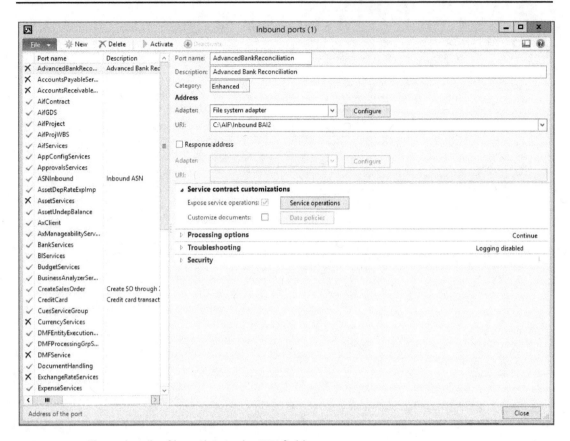

Now you will see that the file path is in the **URI** field.

Next, we need to link the port with the bank services. To do this click on the **Service Operations** button within the **Service Contract Customizations** tab group.

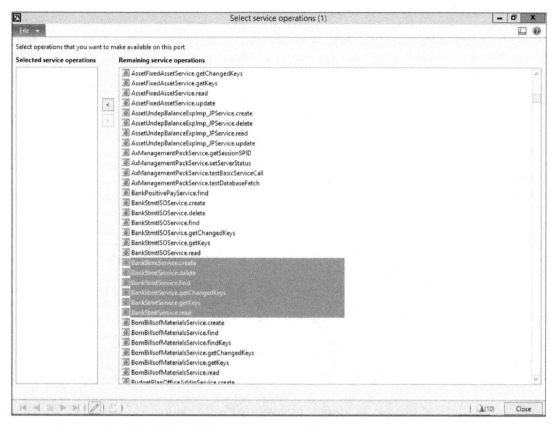

When the **Select Service Operations** dialog box is displayed, select the following service operations and then click on the **<** button to select them:

BankStmtService.create, **BankStmtService.delete**, **BankStmtService.find**,
BankStmtService.getChangedKeys, **BankStmtService.getKeys**, **BankStmtService.**

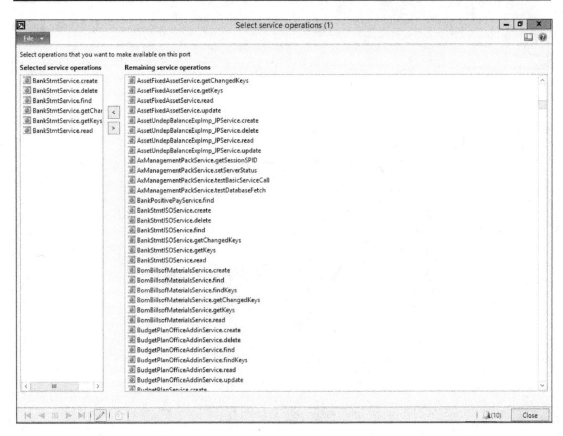

After they have been added to the **Selected Service Operations** click on the **Close** button to exit from the form.

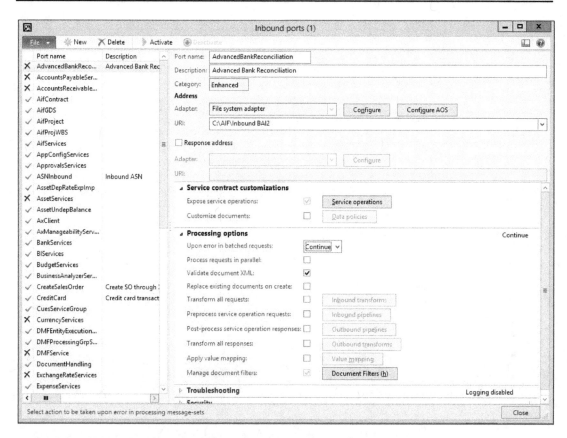

Now expand out the **Processing Options** fast tab group.

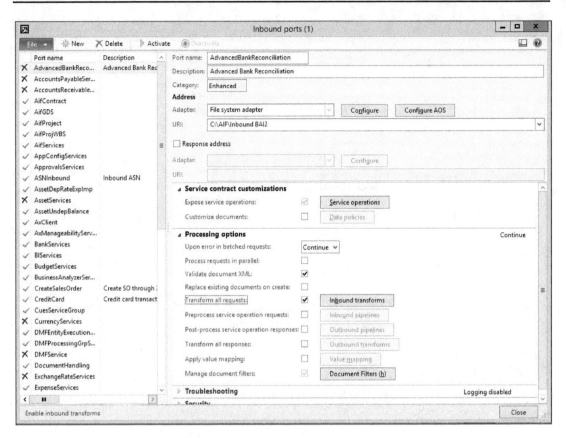

Check the **Transform All Requests** flag and then click on the **Inbound Transforms** button.

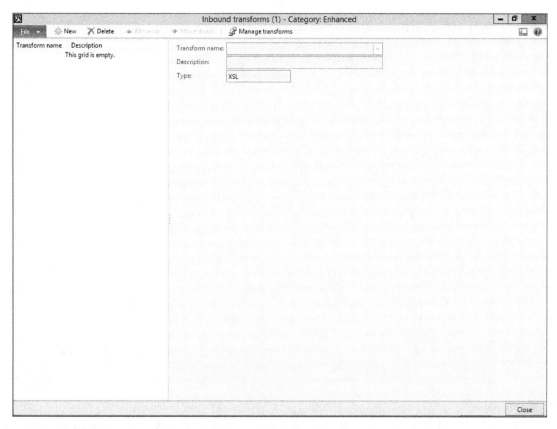

When the **Inbound Transforms** maintenance form is displayed, click on the **New** button to create a new record.

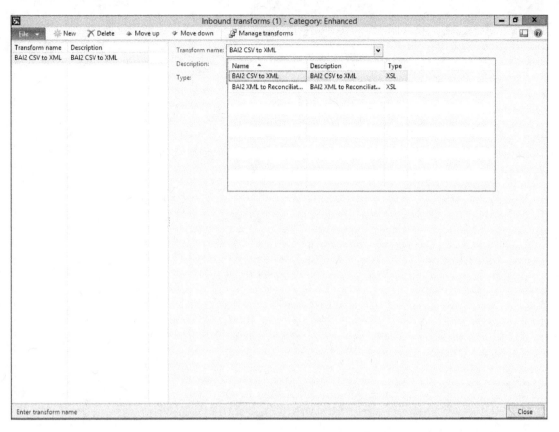

From the **Transform Name** dropdown list, select the **BAI2 CSV to XML** record and press **CTRL+S** to save the record.

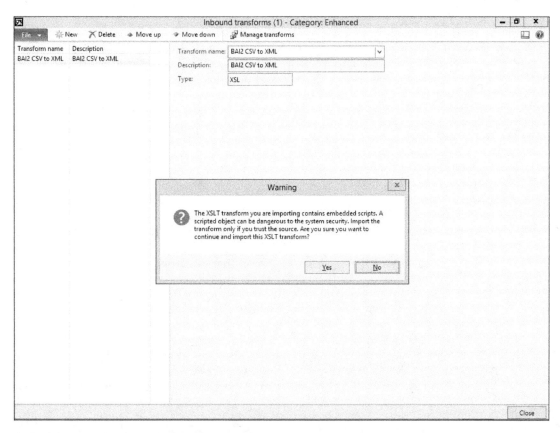

When the warning message is displayed, click on the **Yes** button.

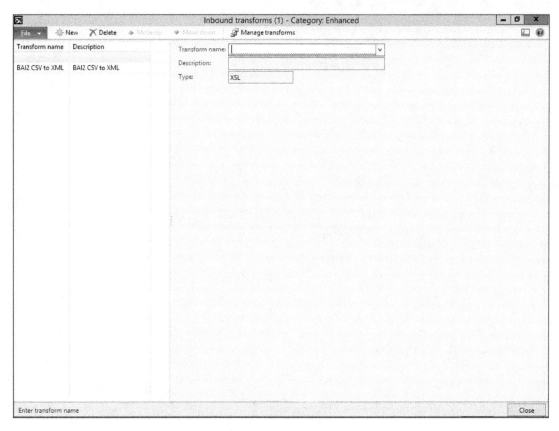

Click on the **New** button again to create another record.

This time, select the **BAI2 XML to Reconciliation** record from the **Transform Name** dropdown list.

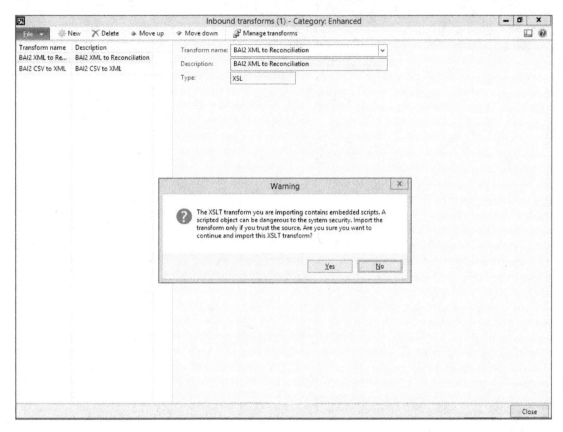

Again, save the record and then click on the **Yes** button when the warning dialog is displayed.

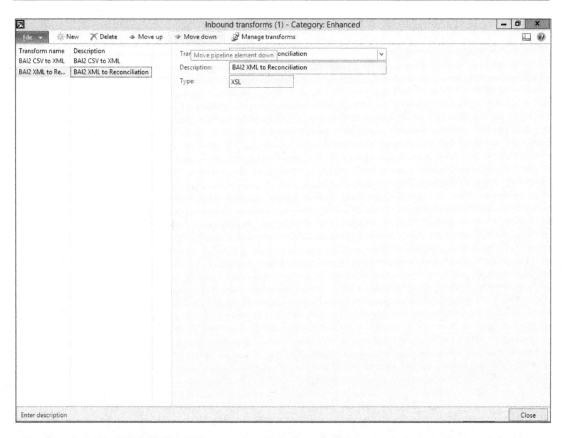

Finally select the **BAI2 CSV to XML** record and click on the **Move Up** button in the menu bar to make this the first transform. This is very important because this sets the order of the transforms and you need to convert the CSV file to XML and then to the Reconciliation format.

After you have done that, click on the **Close** button to exit from the form.

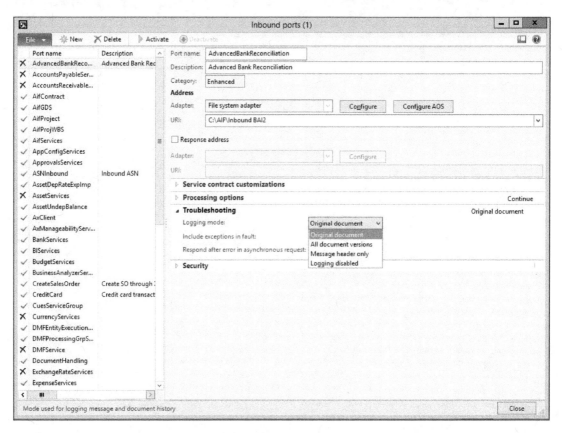

Now expand out the **Troubleshooting** fast tab group and change the **Logging Mode** to **Original Document**.

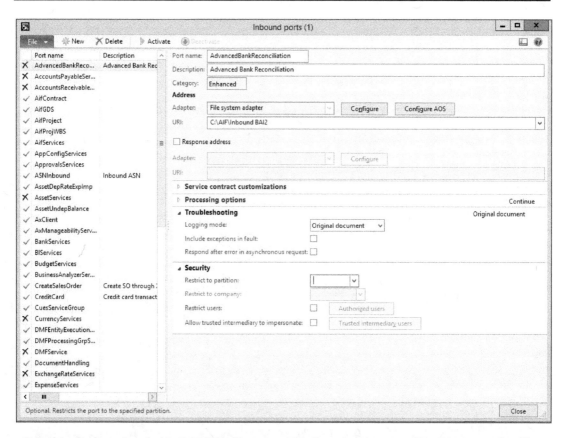

One thing to keep in mind is that AIF will run separately under the users ID, and as a result will chose the default partition and company that the user is assigned to. If you have multiple partitions and/or multiple companies then you may want to specify where you want this reconciliation to run. To do this, expand the **Security** fast tab group.

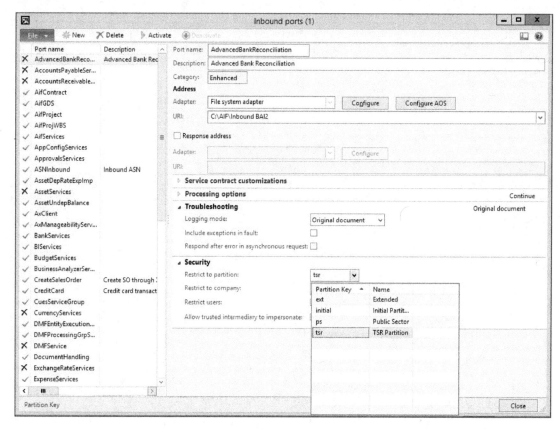

From the **Restrict To Partition** dropdown list select the partition that you want to use.

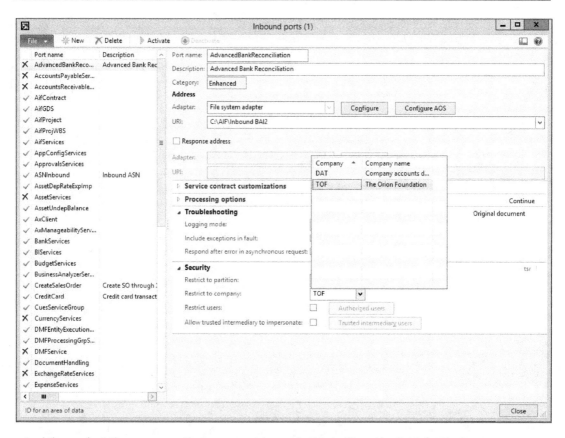

And then select the company that you want to apply this to from the **Restrict To Company** dropdown list.

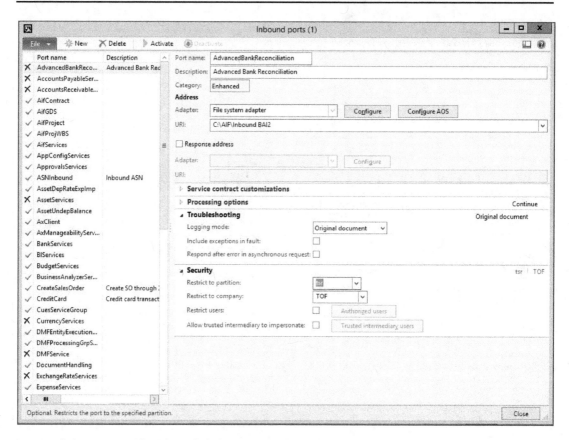

Now all that you need to do is click the **Activate** button in the menu bar to make the port usable by AX.

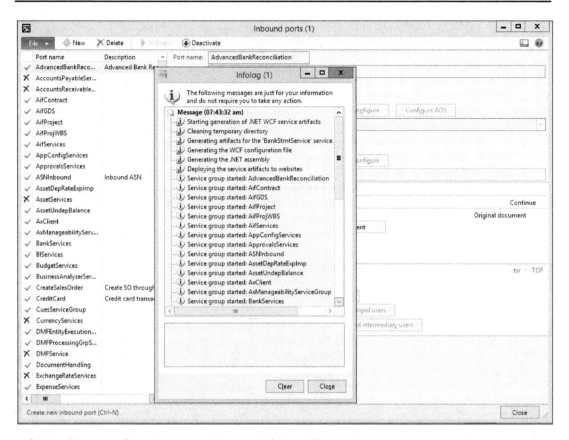

If everything goes fine, then you will get an InfoLog telling you that everything worked great.

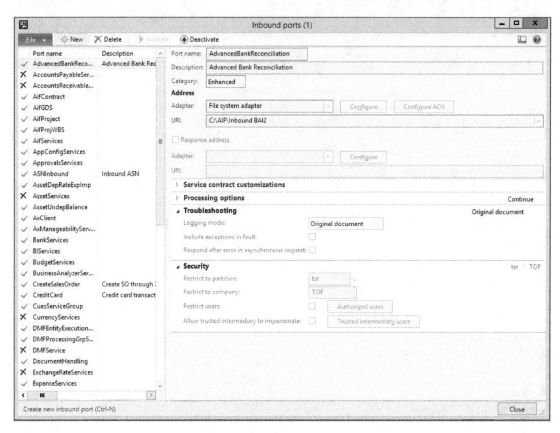

Once that is done, just click on the **Close** button to exit from the form.

Configuring The Bank Statement Format

Now we have all of the building blocks to start configuring our bank statements to use the import feature.

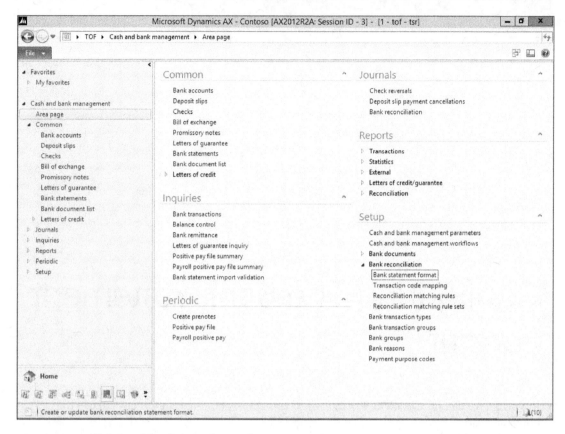

To do start off doing this, click on the **Bank Statement Format** menu item within the **Bank Reconciliation** folder of the **Setup** group within the **Cash And Bank Management** area page.

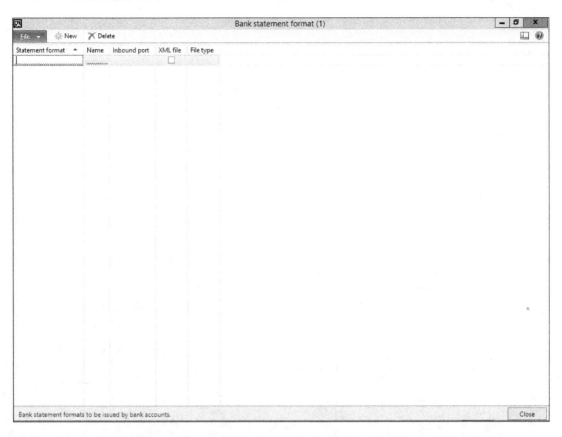

When the **Bank Statement Format** maintenance form is displayed, click on the **New** button within the menu bar to create a new record.

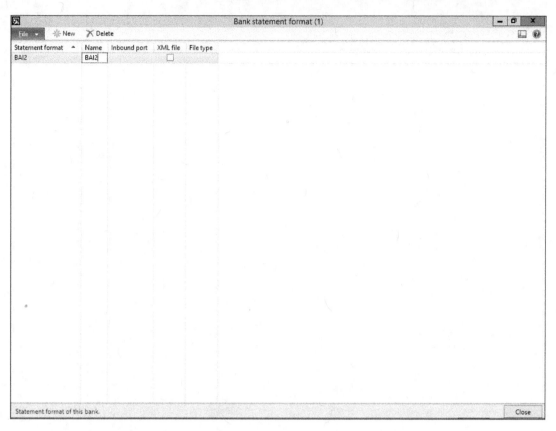

Set the **Statement Format** and the **Name** to **BAI2**.

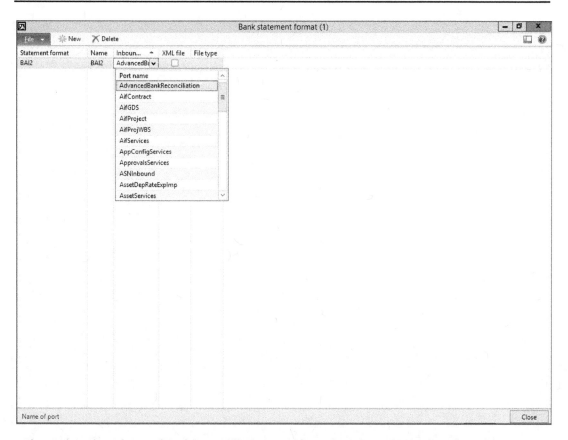

Then select the **AdvancedBankReconciliation** port from the **Inbound Port** dropdown list.

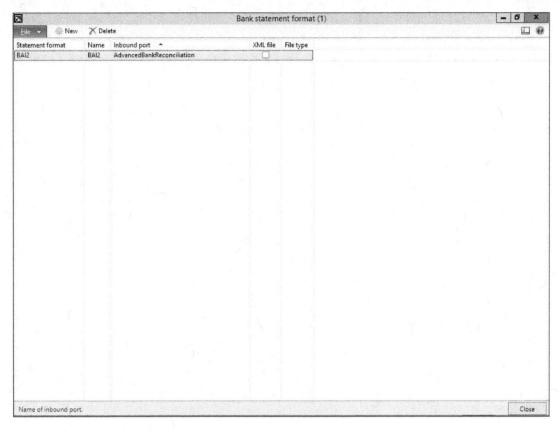

Now just click the **Close** button to exit from the form.

Enabling Advanced Bank Reconciliation On The Bank

The final setup task that we need to perform now is to enable the **Advanced Bank Reconciliation** feature on our bank.

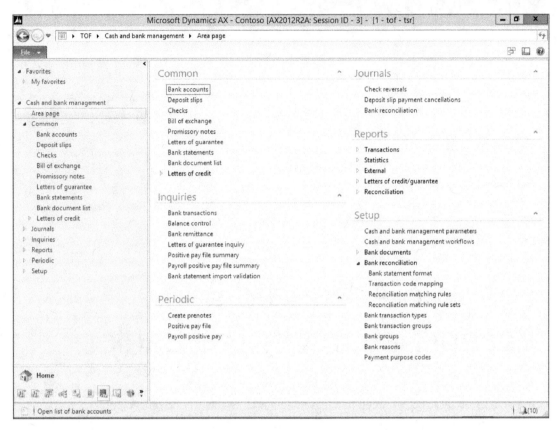

To do this, click on the **Bank Accounts** menu item within the **Common** group of the **Cash And Bank Management** area page.

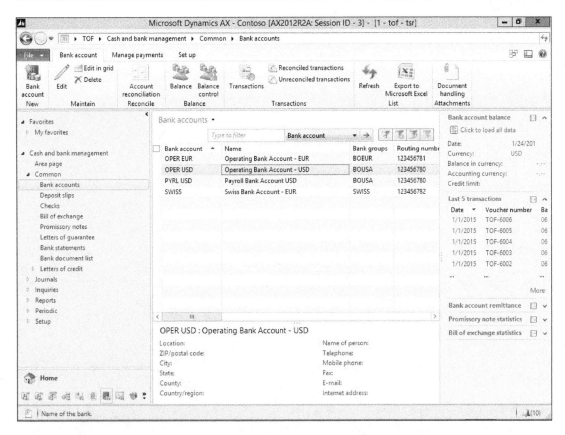

When the **Bank Accounts** list page is displayed, double click on the bank account that you want to use to import your bank statements into.

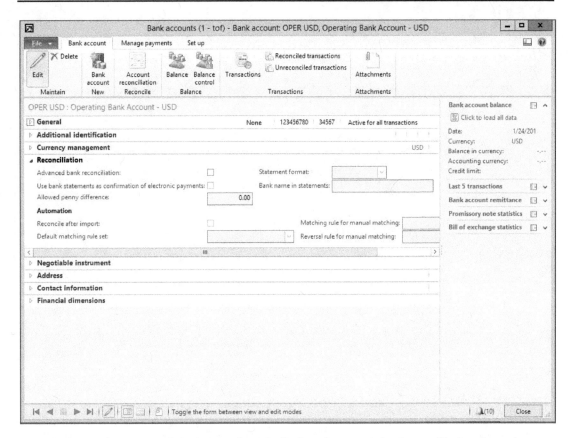

When the **Bank Account** maintenance form is displayed, expand the **Reconciliation** fast tab group and then click the **Advanced Bank Reconciliation** flag.

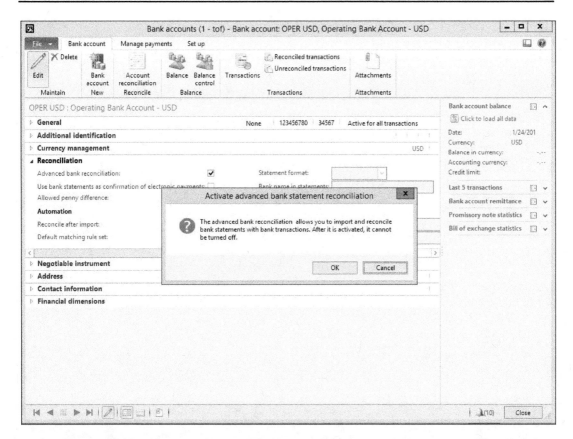

You will get a warning that says that once this is turned on then you cannot turn it off, and click on the **OK** button.

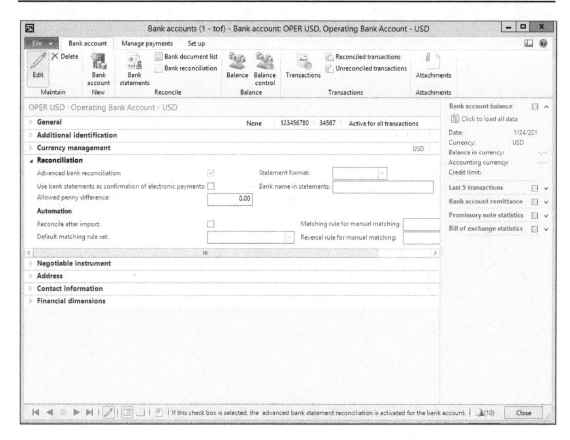

This will enable all of the fields now within the **Reconciliation** fast tab group.

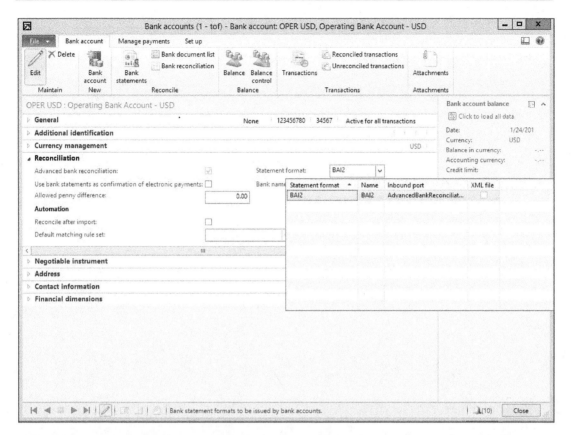

Click on the **Statement Format** dropdown list and select the **BAI2** statement format that you just created and you are done.

Now click on the **Close** button to exit from the form.

Checking The Bank Reconciliation Number Sequences

There is one quick housekeeping matter that you need to check on before we start importing in our bank statements, and that is that the number sequences have been configured for the Advanced Bank Reconciliation.

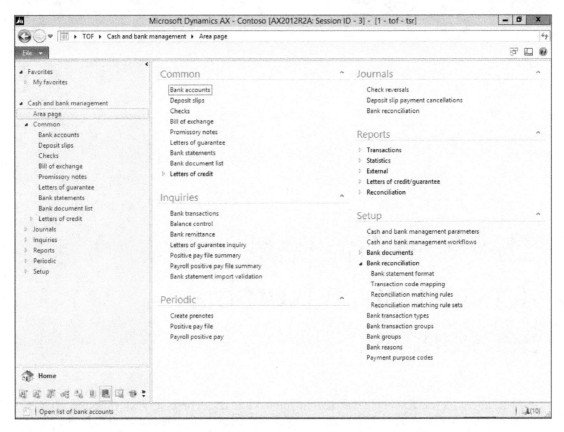

To do this, click on the **Cash And Bank Management Parameters** menu item within the **Setup** group of the **Cash And Bank Management** area page.

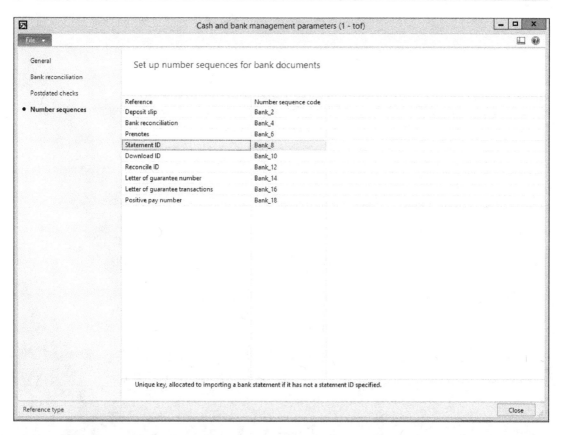

When the **Cash And Bank Management Parameters** maintenance form is displayed, switch to the **Number Sequences** page and make sure that the **Statement ID**, **Download ID**, and **Reconciliation ID** number sequences are configured.

Importing In A Bank Statement File

Now we can import our bank statements.

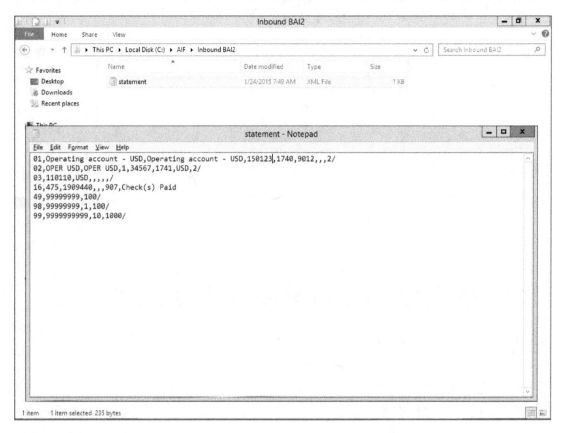

Start off by putting your bank statement files into the **Inbound Port** folder that you created earlier on.

01,Operating account - USD,Operating account - USD,150123,1740,9012,,,2/

02,OPER USD,OPER USD,1,150123,1741,USD,2/

03,110110,USD,,,,,/

16,475,1909440,,,907,Check(s) Paid

49,99999999,100/

98,99999999,1,100/

99,9999999999,10,1000/

Here is a sample one-line BAI2 file.

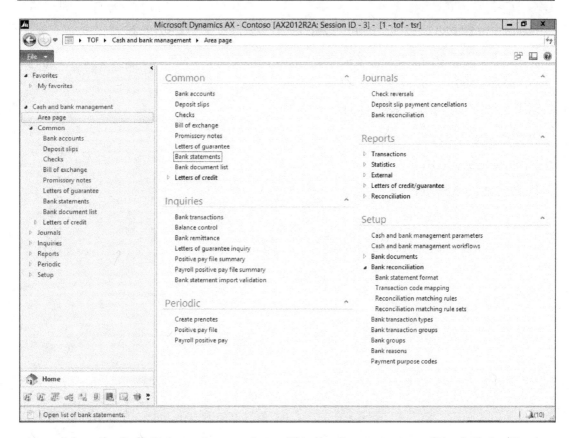

Now click on the **Bank Statements** menu item within the **Common** group of the **Cash And Bank Management** area page.

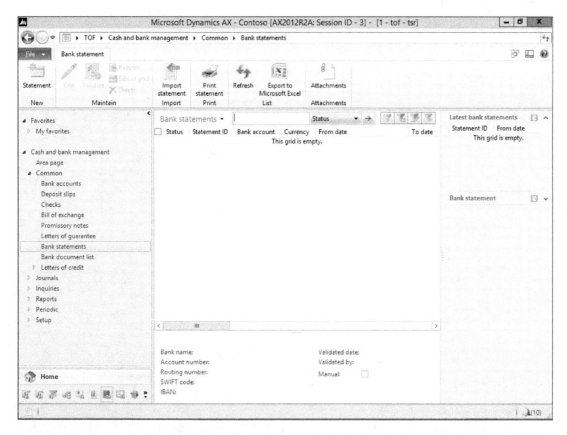

When the **Bank Statements** list page is displayed, click on the **Import Statement** button within the **Import** group of the **Bank Statement** ribbon bar.

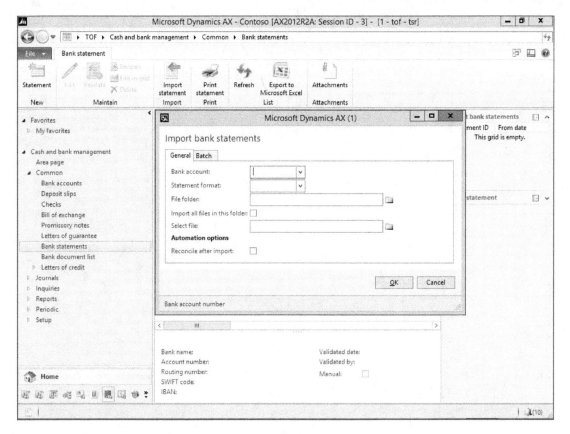

This will open up the **Import Bank Statements** dialog box.

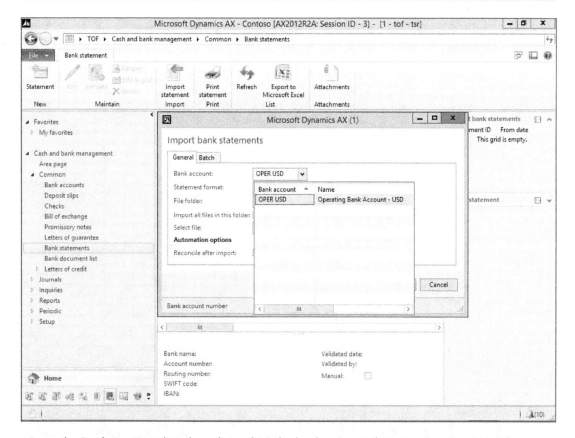

From the **Bank Account** dropdown list, select the bank account that you want to import the statement into. Notice that only the bank accounts that have been enabled for the **Advanced Bank Reconciliation** show up here.

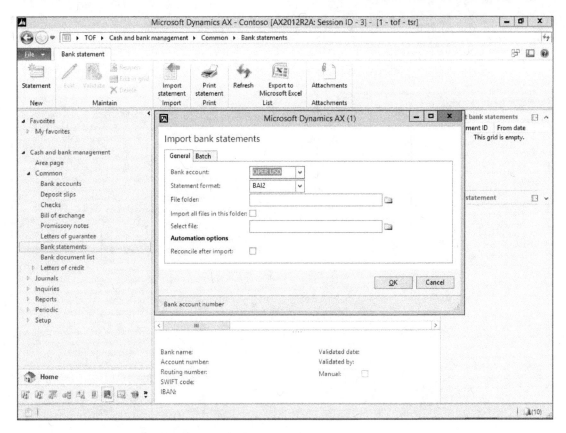

The **Statement Format** will also automatically populate from the **Bank Account**.

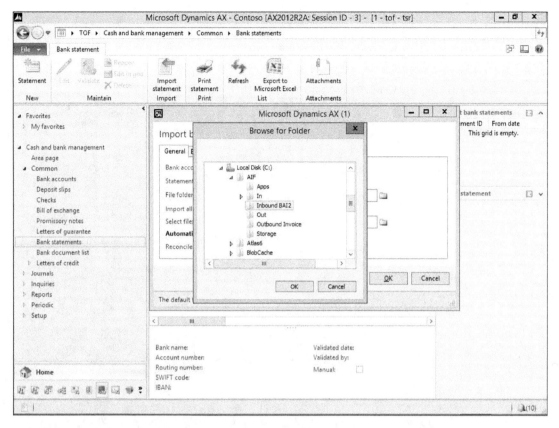

Click on the folder icon to the right of the **File Folder** field and select the inbound ports folder where the bank statements are stored away in.

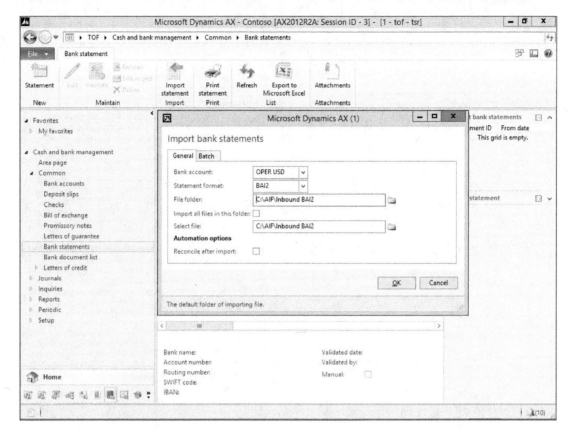

Now click on the folder icon to the right of the **Select File** field.

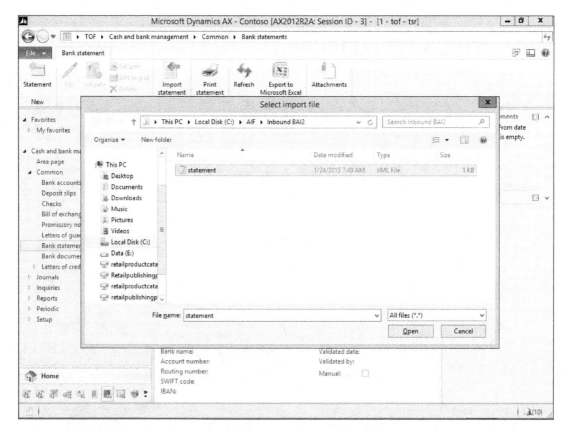

This will allow you to select the individual statement that you want to import and then click on the **Open** button.

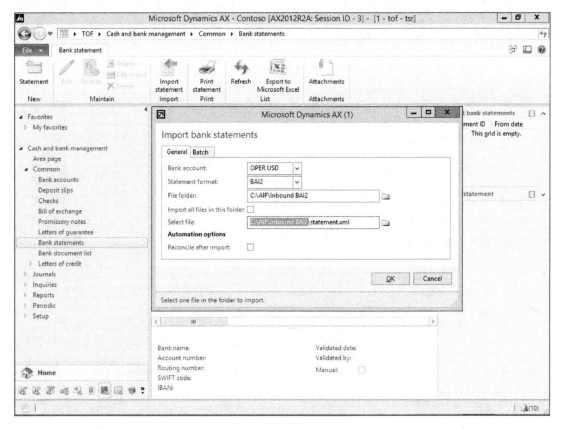

Now all you need to do is click on the **OK** button to start the import.

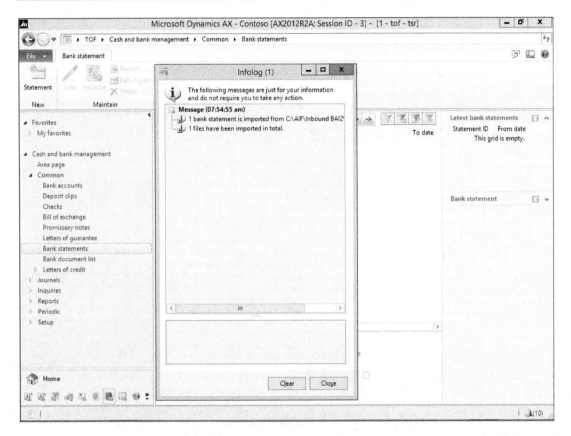

If everything goes well then you will get an InfoLog that says that the statement was loaded.

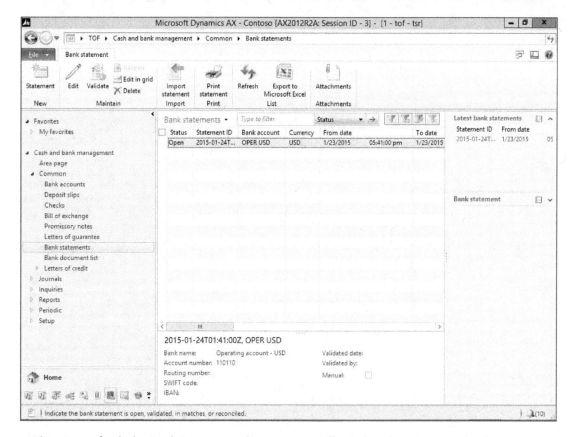

When you refresh the **Bank Statements** list page you will see that there is a new bank statement.

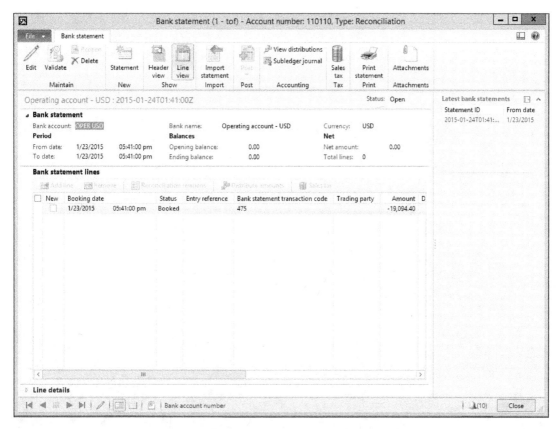

And if you drill into the statement you will see that the detail is also loaded in.

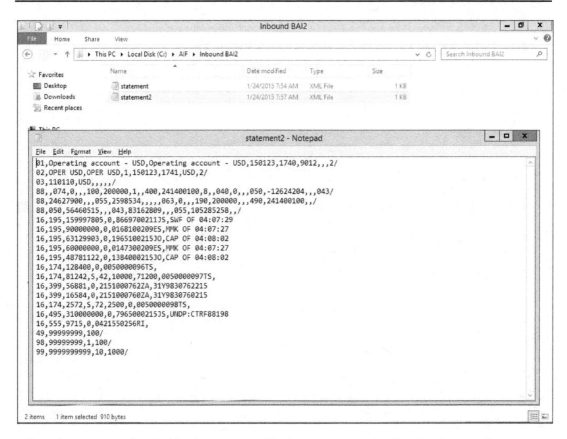

If you have a more detailed bank statement file then you can try loading that in as well.

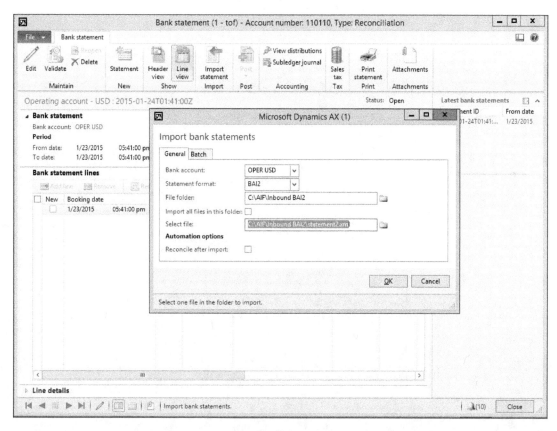

Just run the **Import Bank Statements** function again and point to the other file.

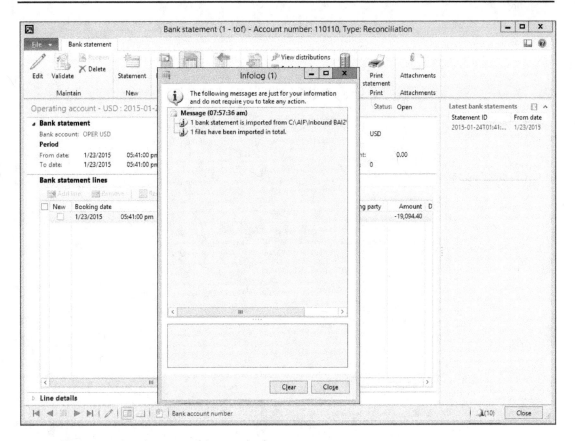

You will get a notice that everything worked out.

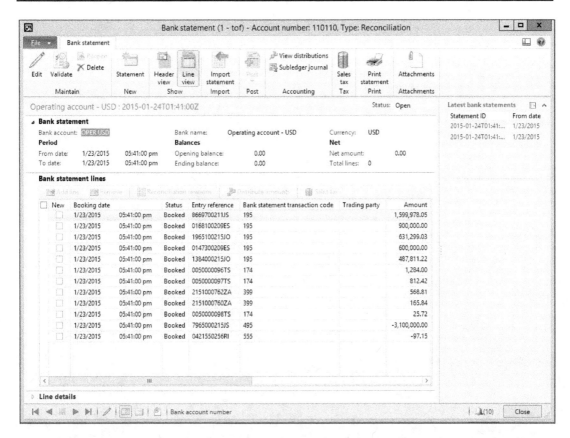

And if you check out the new bank statement that was loaded you will see a lot more detail has been imported in.

Deleting Bank Statements

If you import multiple bank statements that, or you create bank statements that overlap, then don't worry, you can tidy up just by deleting the ones that you don't need – as long as you haven't posted them.

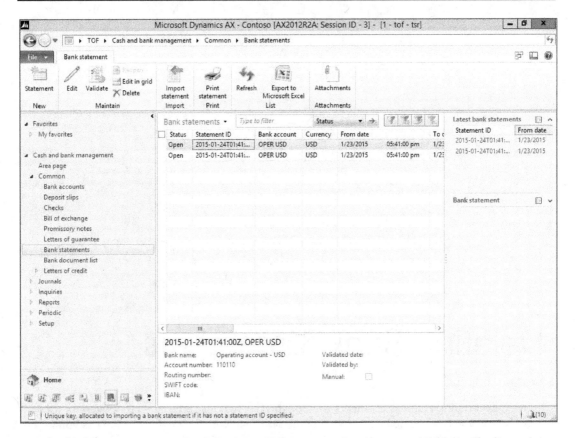

To do this just open up your **Bank Statements** list page, select the record that you don't need and click on the **Delete** button within the **Maintain** group of the **Bank Statement** ribbon bar.

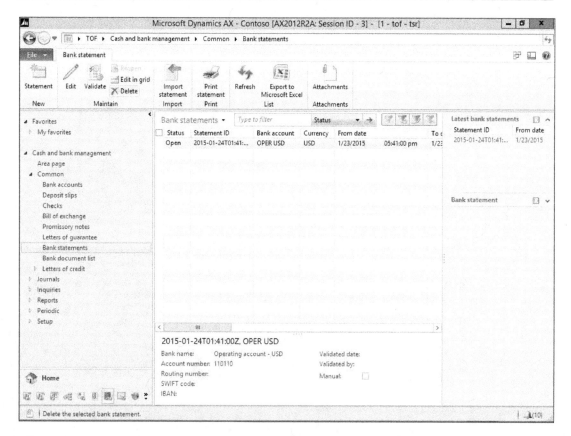

Done.

Validating A Bank Statement

After uploading a **Bank Statement** you may want to double check that all of the data is valid by running the **Validation** process.

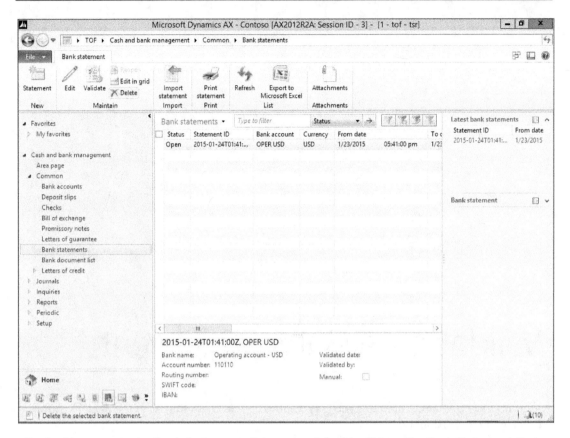

To do this, open up the **Bank Statements** list page and double click on the Bank Statement that you want to validate.

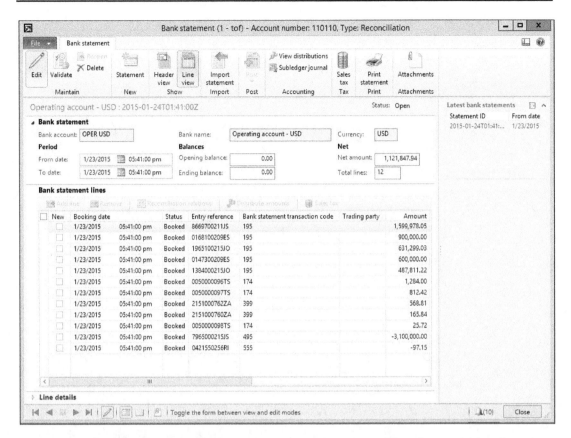

When the **Bank Statement** detail page is displayed, click on the **Validate** button within the **Maintain** group of the **Bank Statement** ribbon bar.

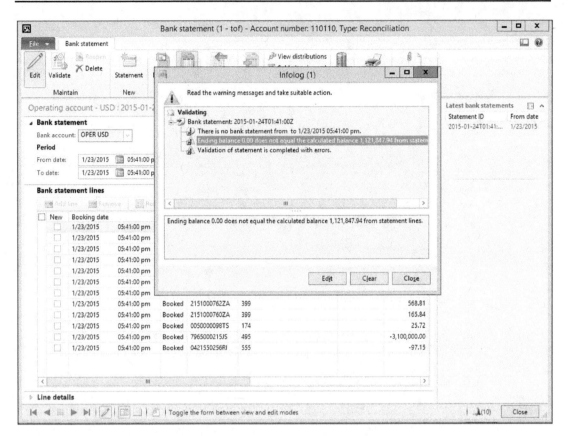

If there are any errors then you will get an InfoLog that lists out what needs to be looked at. In this case our statement dates are a little off and our balances don't match.

Click on the **Close** button to exit from the form.

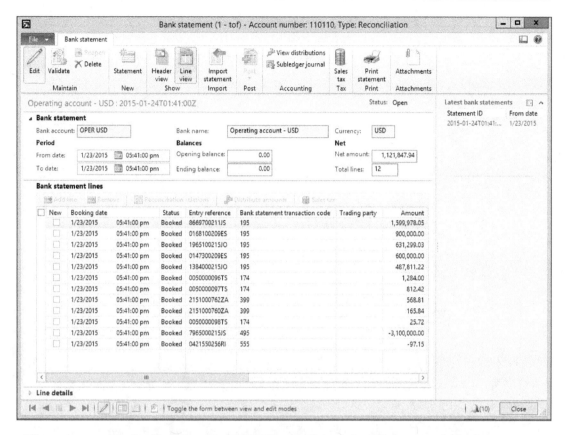

When we return to the **Bank Statement** detail page click on the **Edit** button within the **Maintain** group of the **Bank Statement** ribbon bar.

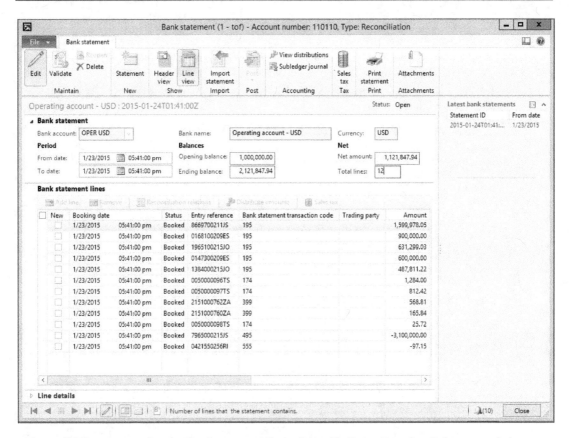

That will allow you to change the Statement **From Date**, **To Date**, **Opening Balance**, and also the **Ending Balance.**

Once you have done that, click on the **Validate** button again.

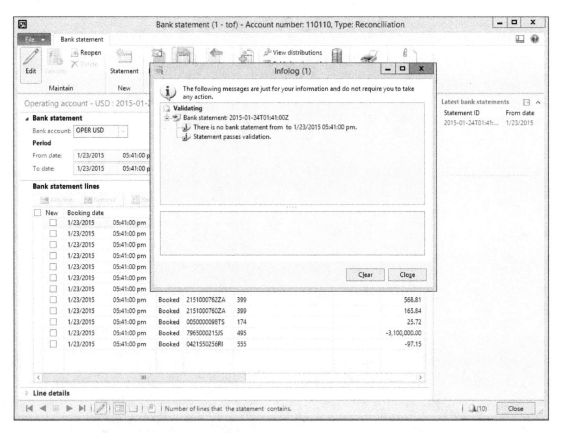

If everything is OK then you will get an InfoLog telling you that.

Posting A Bank Statement

Once you have validated your bank statement, you can close it out by posting it to the ledger and the bank.

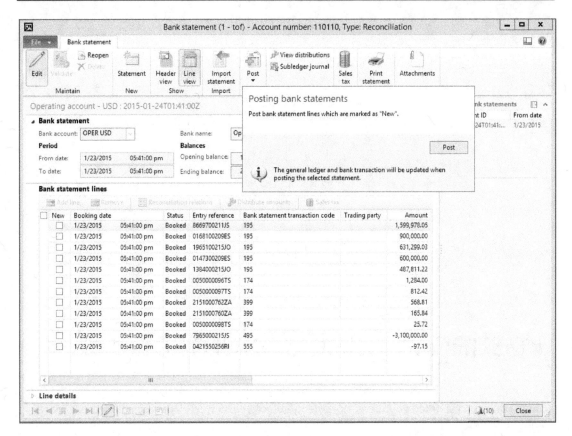

To do this, just click on the **Post** button within the **Post** group of the **Bank Statement** ribbon bar and click on the **Post** button.

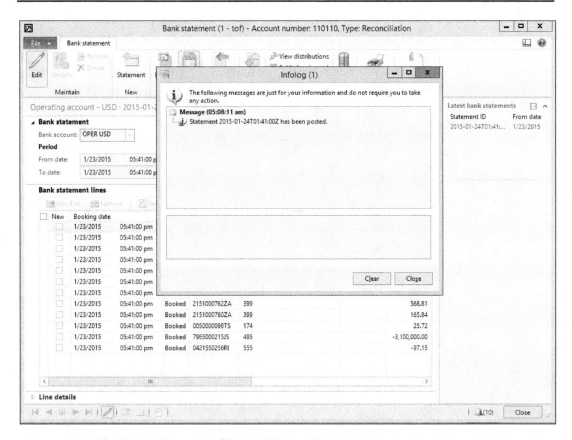

If everything is OK you will get an InfoLog telling you that the statement has been posted.

Configuring Bank Code Transaction Mappings

The codes that you use within Dynamics AX for coding your bank statement lines may not necessarily be the same as the ones that the bank use when they send you the bank statements. Don't worry, because you can easily configure a mapping between the banks transaction codes and yours.

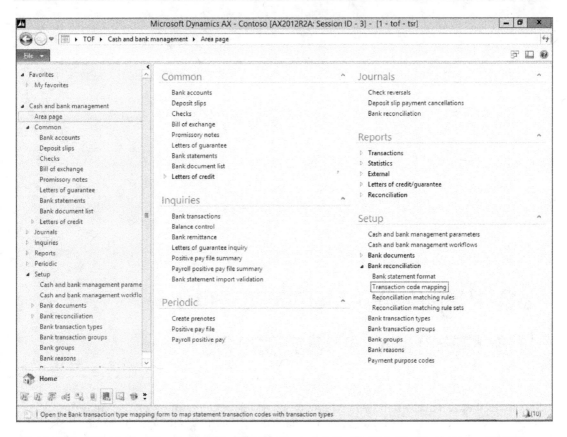

To do this, click on the **Transaction Code Mapping** menu item within the **Bank Reconciliation** folder of the **Setup** group within the **Cash and Bank Management** area page.

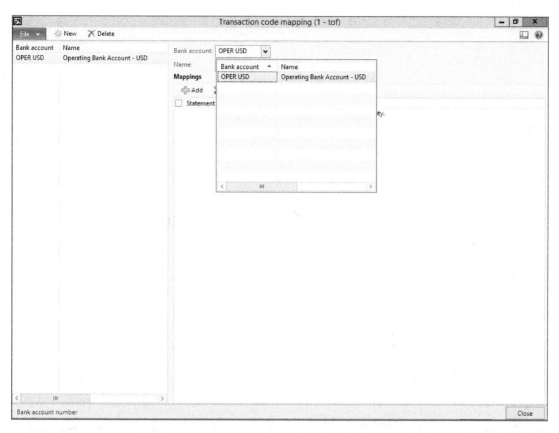

When the **Transaction Code Mapping** maintenance form is displayed, click on the **New** button in the menu bar to create a new record and then click on the **Bank Account** dropdown list to select he bank account that you want to set up the mapping for. In this case we will select **OPER USD**.

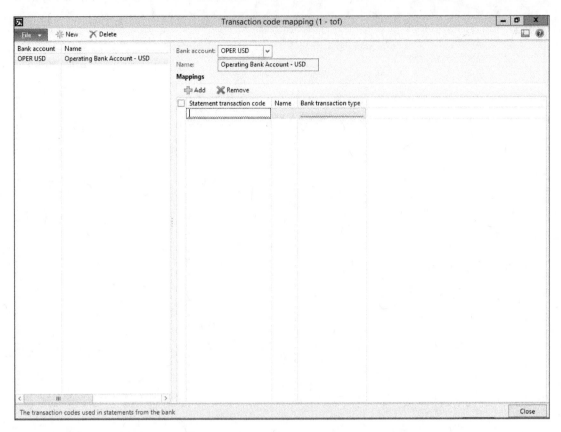

Then within the **Mapping** table, click on the **Add** button to insert a new mapping line.

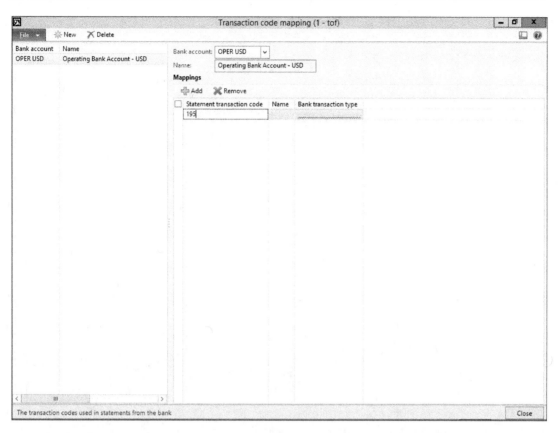

Enter in the banks transaction code that you want to translate. For example **195**.

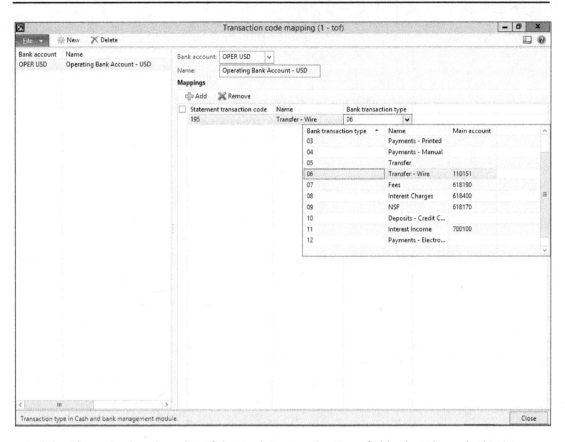

And then from the dropdown list of the **Bank Transaction Type** field select the code that it translates to. In this example it's **06**.

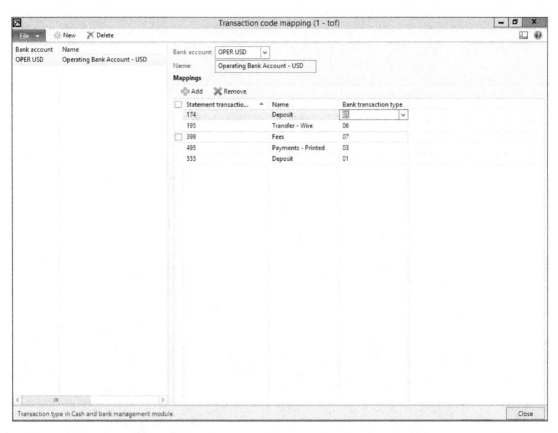

Repeat the process for all of the other Statement Codes and when you are done click on the **Close** button to exit from the form.

Using The Advanced Bank Reconciliation Worksheet

Once you have imported in the Bank Statement to can use the Advanced Bank Reconciliation Worksheet form to match all of your transactions and clear out the accounts.

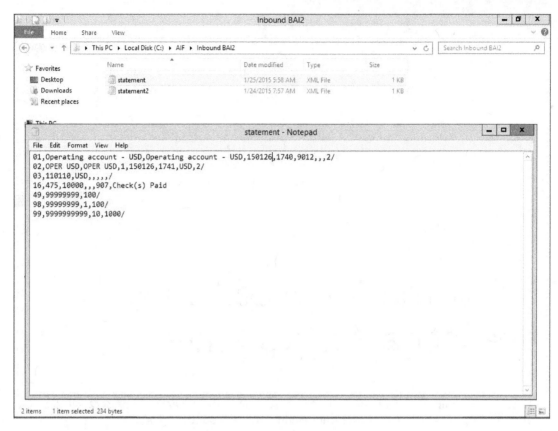

To do this we will start off with a new statement file.

Open up the **Bank Statements** list page and click on the **Import Statement** button within the **Import** group of the **Bank Statement** ribbon bar.

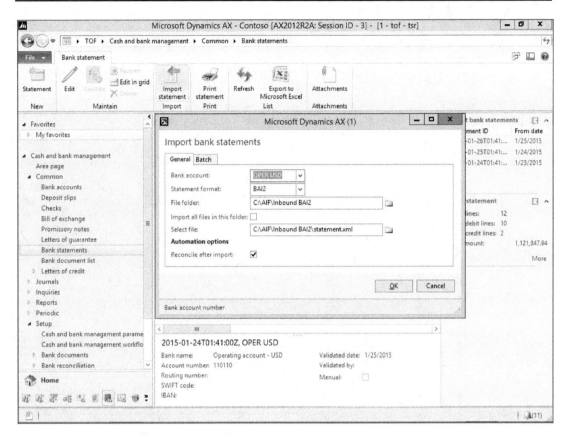

When the **Import Bank Statement** dialog box is displayed, make any changes to the file name or location and then click on the **OK** button.

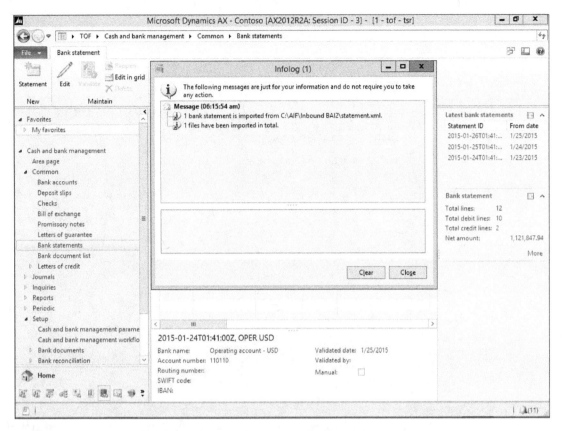

When the import InfoLog is displayed, click on the **Close** button.

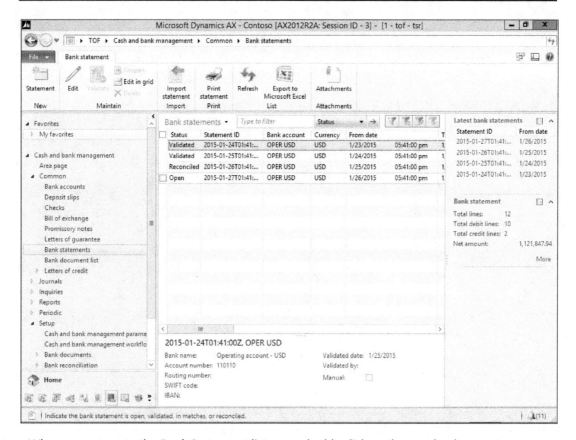

When you return to the **Bank Statement** list page, double click on the new bank statement.

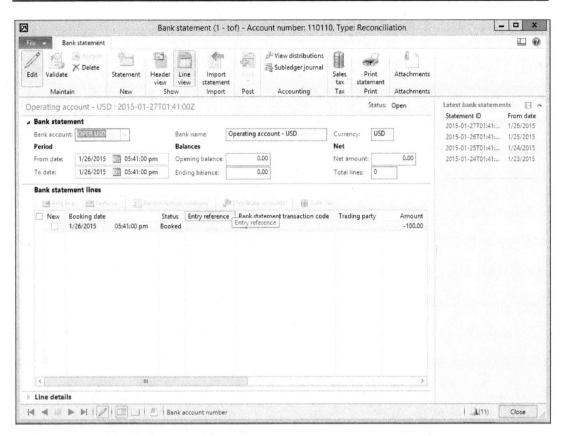

When the **Bank Statement** detail form is displayed, click on the **Edit** button to switch to edit mode.

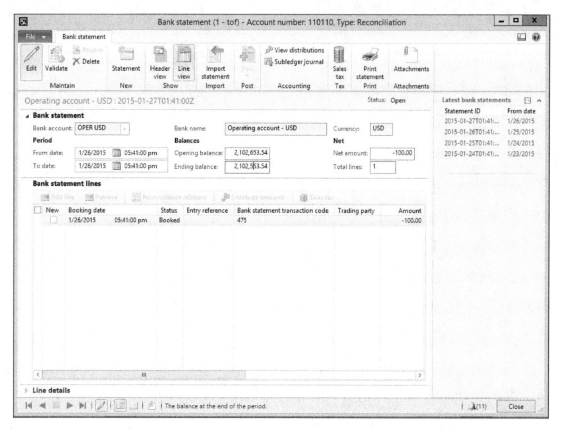

This will allow you to modify the starting and ending balances and also the to and from dates if necessary.

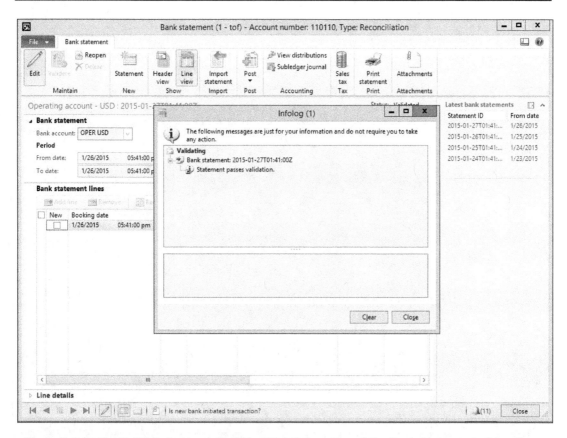

Then click on the **Validate** button within the **Maintain** group of the **Bank Statement** ribbon bar. Make sure that everything is OK and close out of the InfoLog.

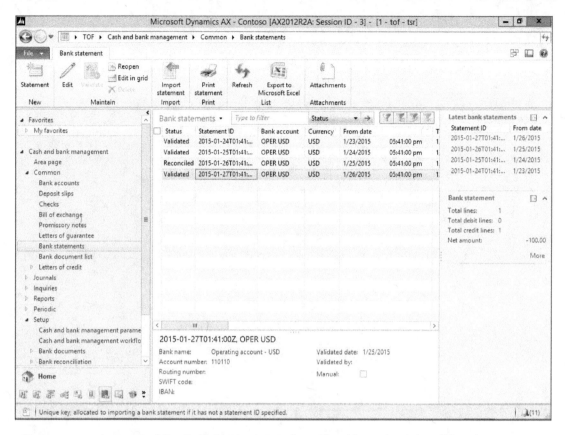

Now you can close out of the **Bank Statement** and you should see that it is validated.

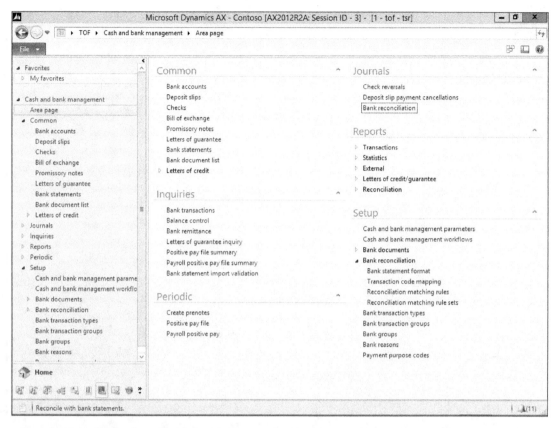

Now click on the **Bank Reconciliation** menu item within the **Journals** group of the **Cash and Bank Management** area page.

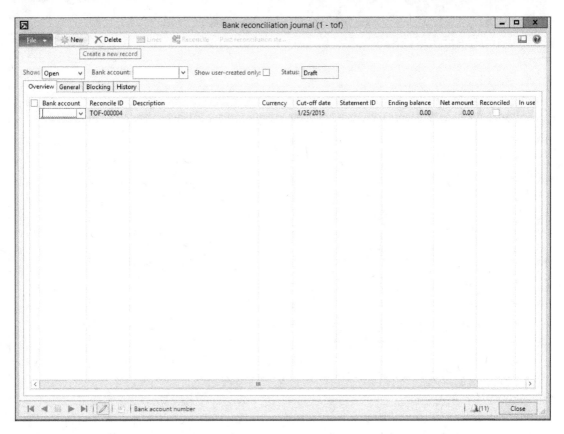

When the **Bank Reconciliation** list page is displayed, click on the **New** button in the menu bar to create a new record.

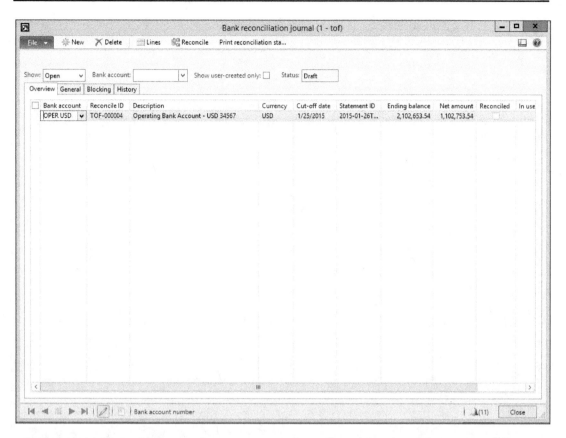

Then enter in the **Bank Account** that you want to reconcile and match. In this case we will use **OPER USD**. After you have done that, click on the **Reconcile** button in the menu bar.

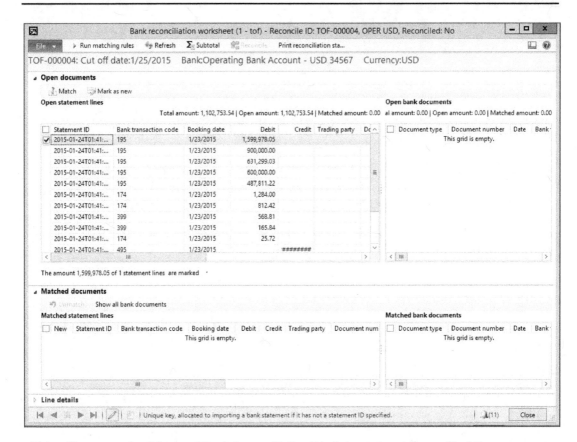

This will open up the Advanced Bank Reconciliation Worksheet showing you all of the statement lines and also any bank documents that are within the system.

Note: Right now the cupboards are a little bare because we have not set up AR or AP.

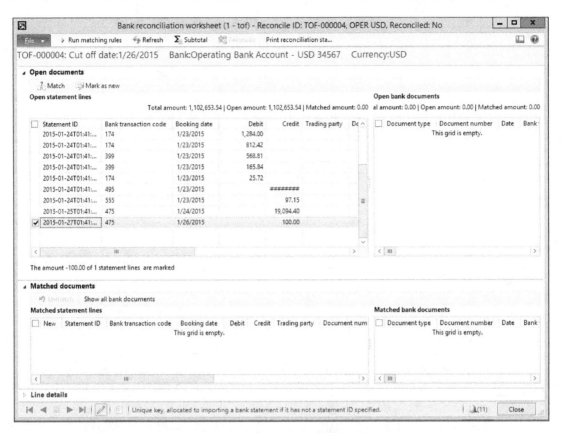

If you scroll down to the bottom of the list of **Open Statement Lines** you will see that our transaction that we just imported is listed there. To approve it and post it as a new bank statement line, select the record and click on the **Mark As New** button within the **Open Documents** header area.

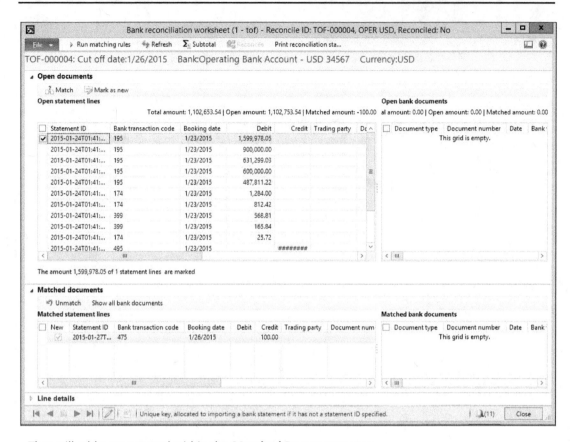

That will add a new record within the **Matched Documents** area.

You can continue matching the statement lines, and when you are done, click on the **Close** button to exit from the form.

Submitting Reconciled Statements for Approval

Once you have reconciled the Bank Statements you can now submit it for approval through the workflow that was created at the beginning of this chapter.

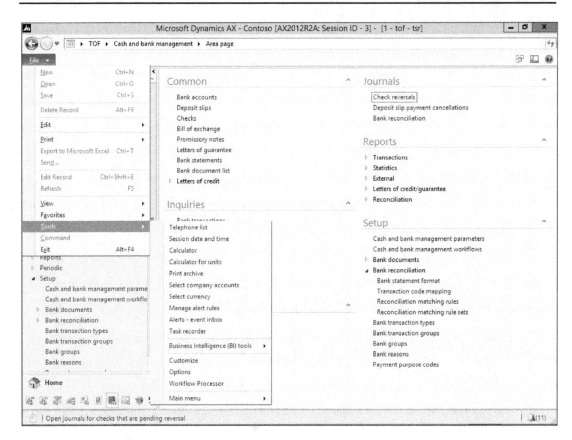

Before we do that though you will probably need to do one thing, and that is to start the Workflow Processor that co-ordinates all of the workflow tasks. If the real world this would be set to run in the background, but if you are using the demonstration environment then you may need to start this up by hand. To do this click on the **Files** menu, select the **Tools** submenu, and click on the **Workflow Processor** menu item.

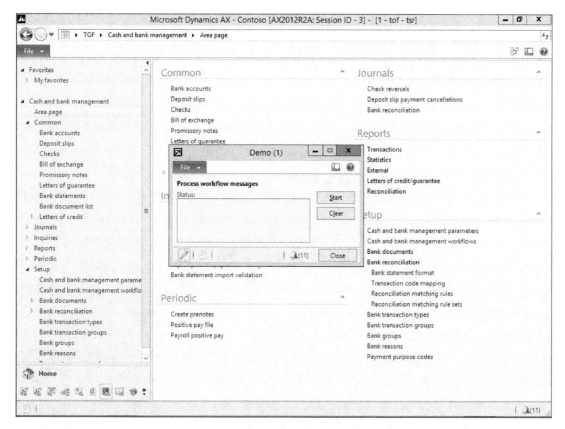

This will open up the **Workflow Processor** and all you need to do is click on the **Start** button.

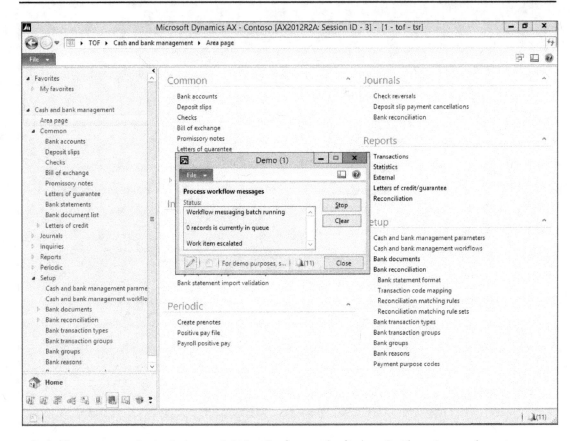

Once the processor is started up, minimize the form – don't close it otherwise you have to reopen it again.

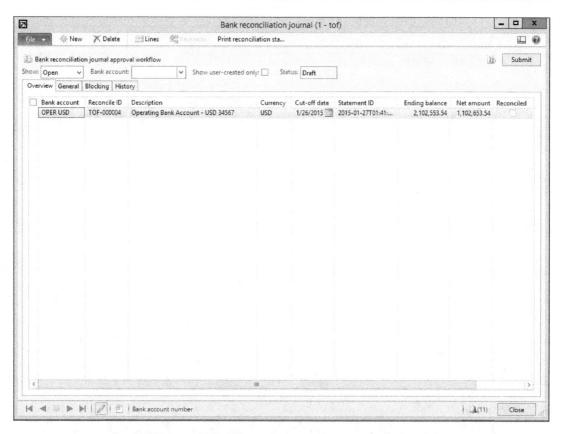

When you return to the **Bank Statements** list page you will see a workflow alert bar is being displayed – this is because you have a configured workflow. Also you will notice that the **Reconcile** option has been disabled, because you need to approve the statement before you are allowed to click on this. To start the workflow approval process off just click on the **Submit** button.

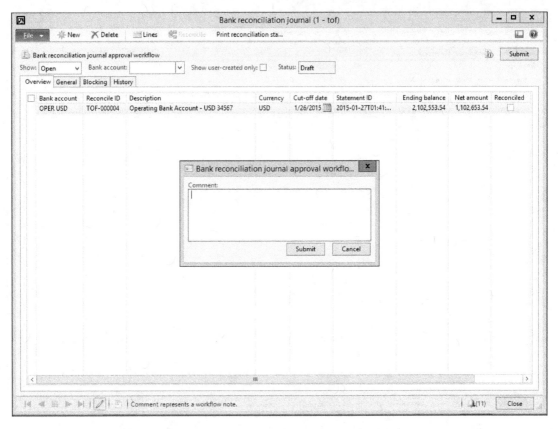

This will open up a dialog box to confirm that you want to submit the statement for approval.

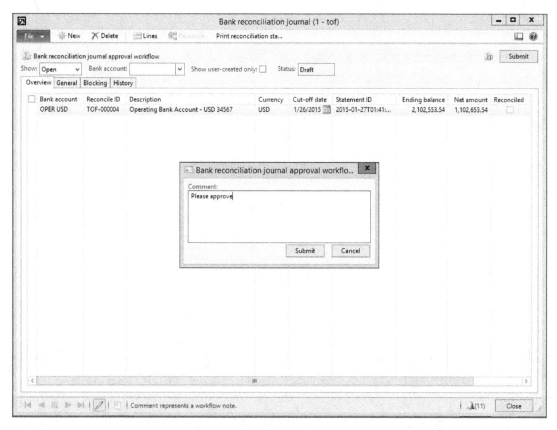

Type in any comments that you may want to add and then click n the **Submit** button.

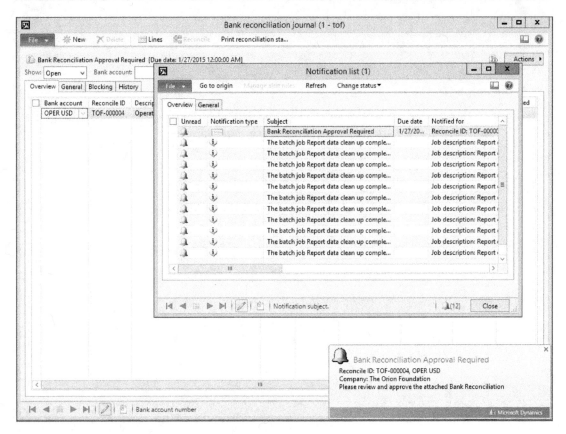

The person that has been assigned to perform the approval will then get a number of notices saying that there is a workflow task that they need to perform.

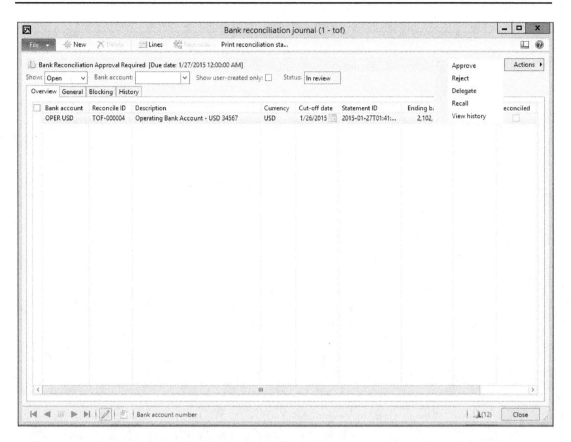

All they need to do is click on the alert which will take them to the transaction, click on the **Actions** button within the workflow tool bar and select the action that they want to take. To approve it, just select the **Approve** button.

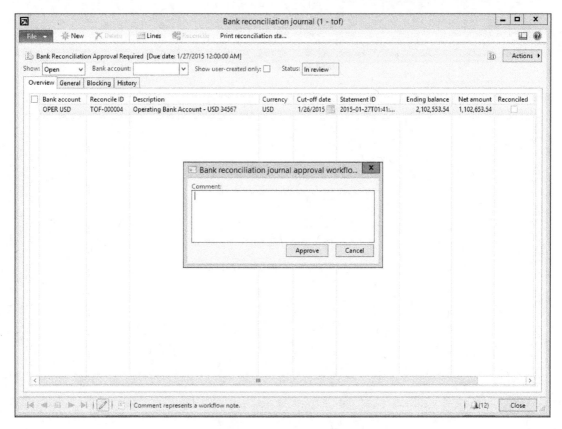

This will open up another comment dialog box for the approval step.

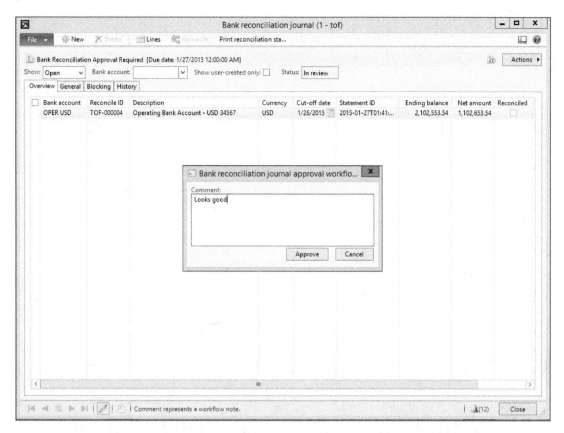

The approver can add any comments that they like and then click on the **Approve** button.

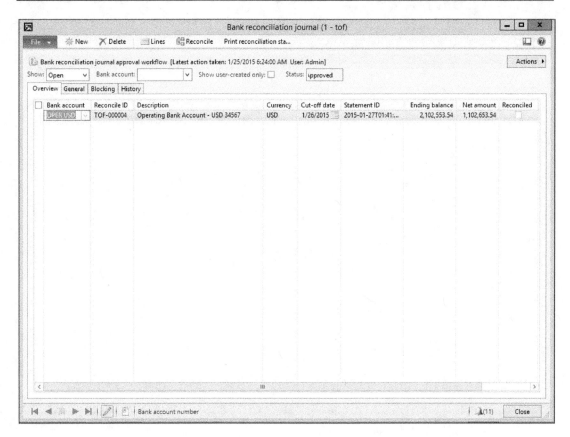

After the workflow process has completed, you will see that the **Reconcile** option is now enabled.

Printing A Reconciliation Statement

If you want to review the bank statement and the reconciled transactions then you can easily do this just by printing out the Reconciliation Statement.

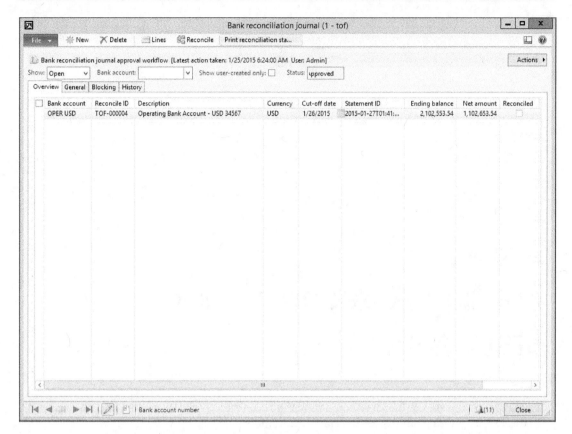

To do this, open up the **Bank Statements** list page, select the statement that you want to print the report for and click on the **Print Reconciliation Statement** button within the menu bar.

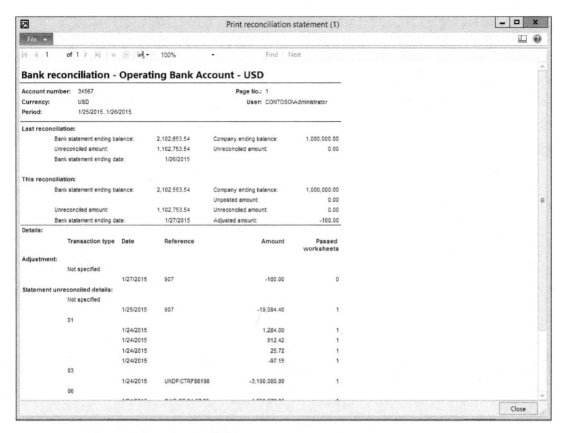

Now you can see all of the reconciliation detail.

Marking a Statement as Reconciled

Once you arte happy with the Bank Statement and it has passed through all of the approval processes you can mark it as reconciled.

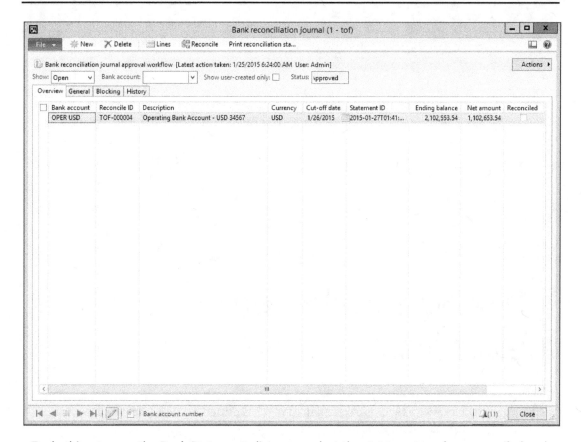

To do this, open up the **Bank Statements** list page, select the statement mark as reconciled and then click on the **Reconcile** button within the menu bar.

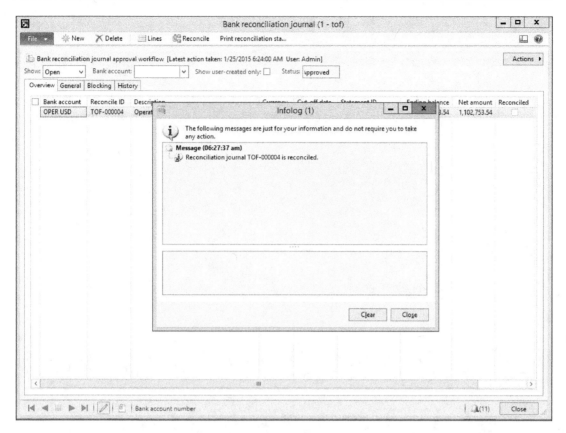

You will get an InfoLog saying that the statement has been reconciled.

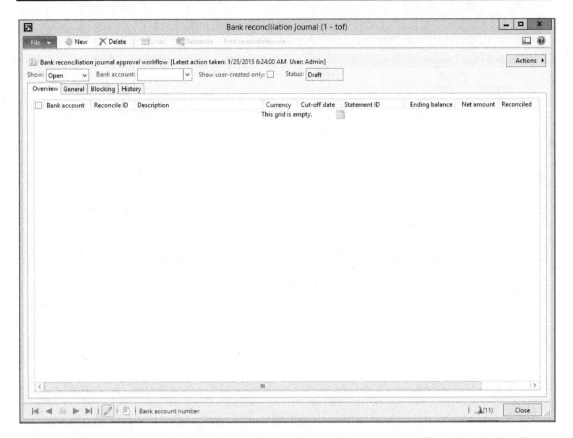

Then when you return to the **Bank Reconciliation Journal** list page you will see that the bank statement has disappeared.

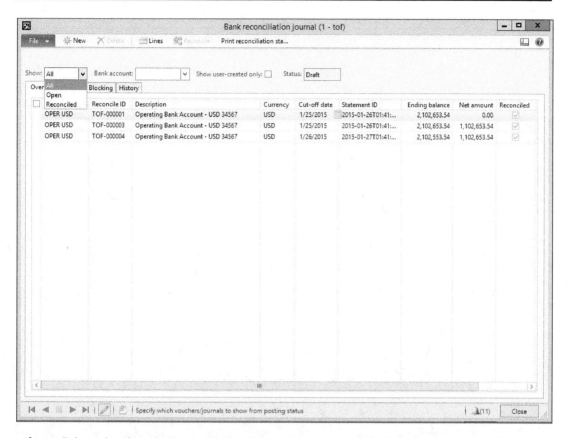

If you click on the **Show** button in the header and then select the **All** option then you will see that it is still there, it has just been filed away.

Posting A Reconciled Bank Statement

Once you have reconciled your bank statement then you can Post it to the ledger.

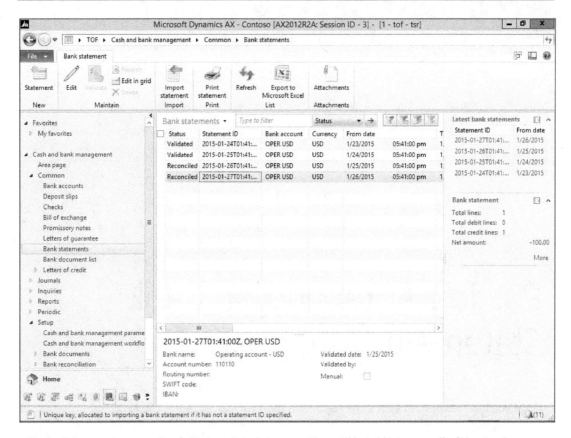

To do this open up your **Bank Statements** list page. You will be able to see all of the Bank Statements that you have reconciled will have the status of **Reconciled**. Double click on the statement that you want to post.

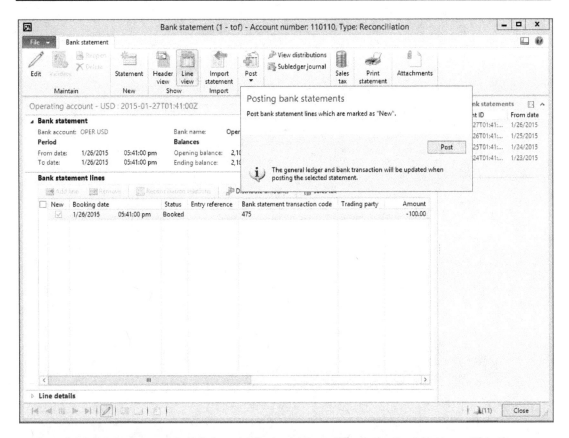

When the **Bank Statement Detail** form is displayed, just click on the **Post** button within the **Post** group of the **Bank Statement** ribbon bar and click on the **Post** button.

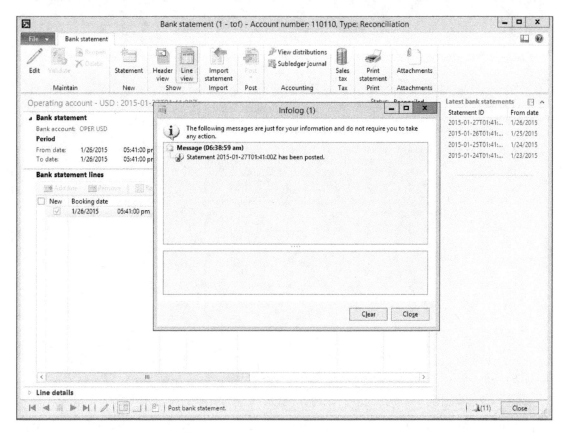

You will then get an InfoLog telling you that statement has been posted and you are done.

Configuring Reconciliation Matching Rules

If you want you can take the reconciliation process to the next level by configuring the automatic matching rules within Dynamics AX. This allows you to define rules and conditions that the system will use to try to automatically tie transactions together directly from the bank statements.

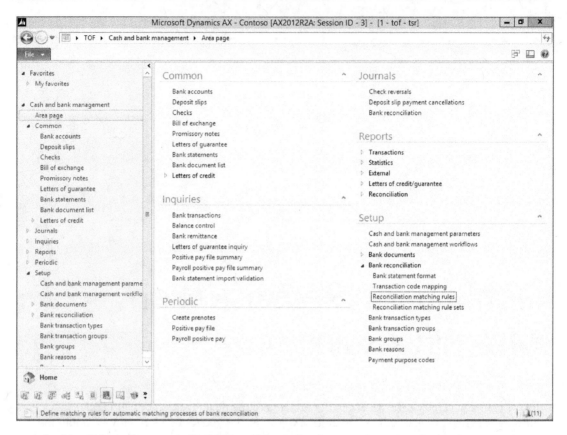

To do this, click on the **Reconciliation Matching Rules** menu item within the **Bank Reconciliation** folder of the **Setup** group within the **Cash and Bank Management** area page.

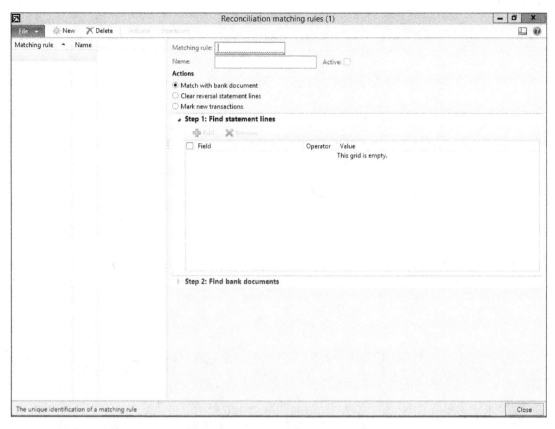

When the **Reconciliation Marching Rules** maintenance form is displayed, click on the **New** button within the menu bar to create a new record.

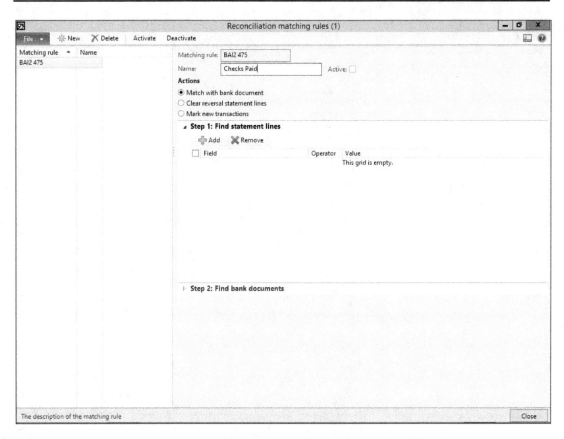

Then set the **Matching Rule** code and **Name**. We will create a rule BAI2 475 with a name of Checks Paid.

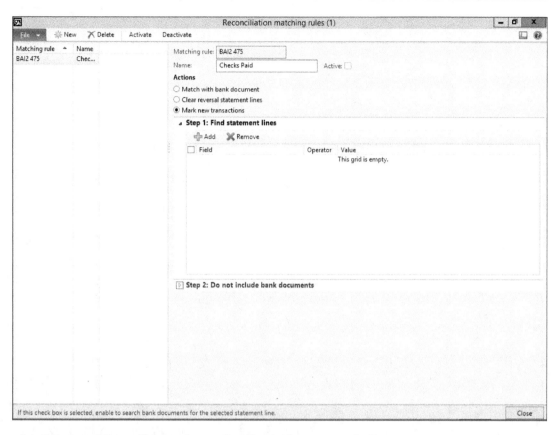

For this example we will just create a simple rule that automatically creates new transactions by setting the **Actions** option to **Mark New Transactions**.

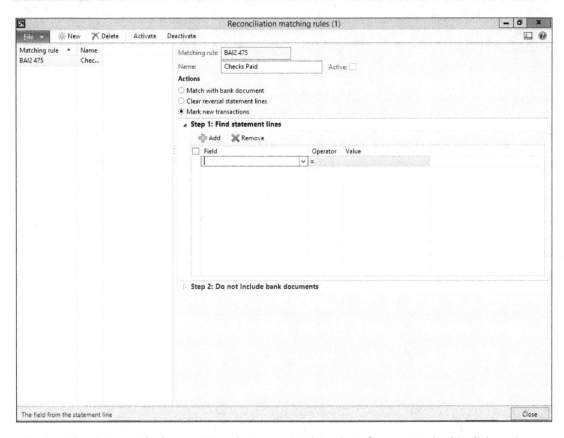

Next we need to specify the condition that we want this rule to fire on. To do this click on the **Add** button within the **Find Statement Lines** tab group.

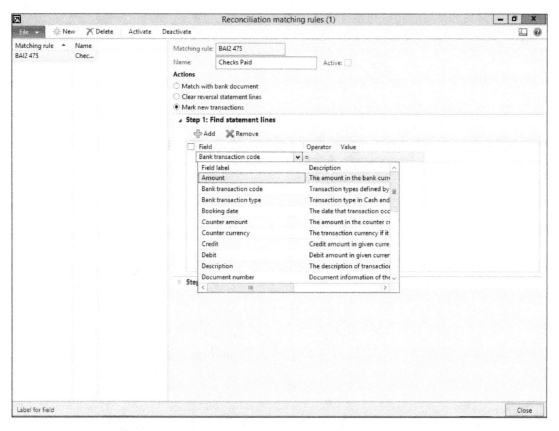

Click on the **Field** dropdown list and select the **Bank Transaction Code** field.

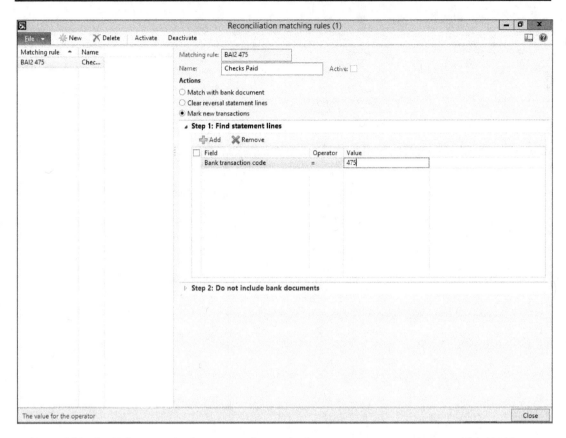

Then within the **Value** type in the transaction code that we want to match to – which in this example will be **475**.

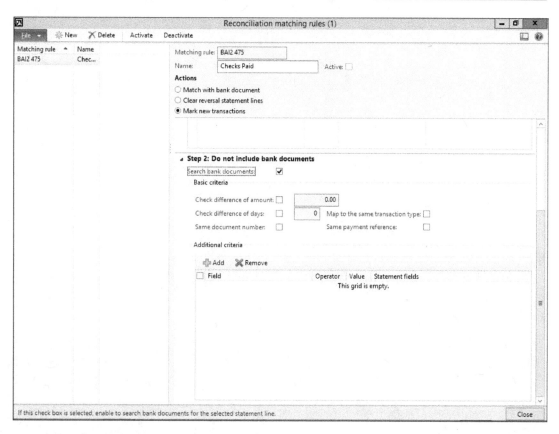

Now expand the **Step 2** tab group.

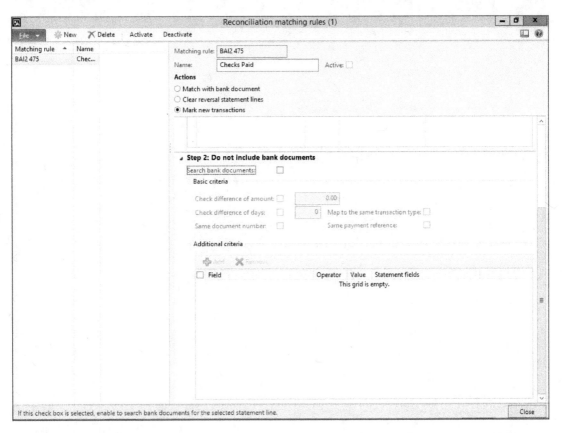

Uncheck the **Search Bank Document** option because this will be an automatic transaction that does not need to be matched.

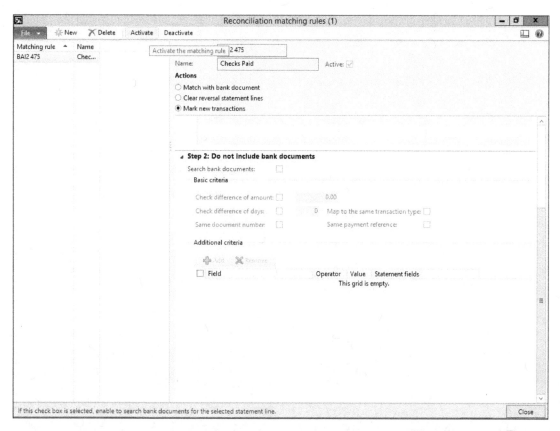

After you are done, click on the **Activate** button within the menu bar to activate it.

Configuring Automatic Matching Rule Sets

Once we have configured our Matching Rules we need to add them to a **Matching Rule Set** so that we can match transactions in groups of rules.

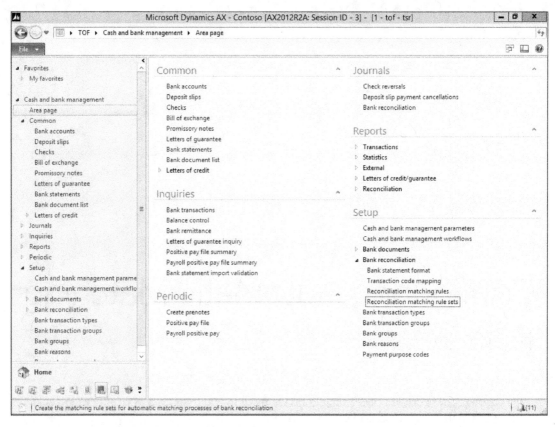

To do this click on the **Reconciliation Matching Rule Sets** menu item within the **Bank Reconciliation** folder of the **Setup** group within the **Cash and Bank Management** area page.

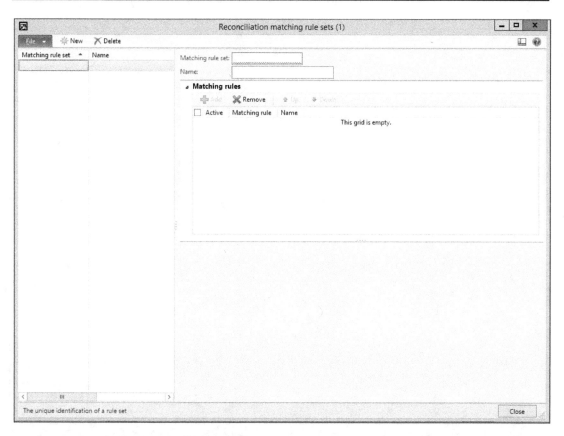

When the **Reconciliation Matching Rule Sets** maintenance form is displayed, click on the **New** button to add a new record.

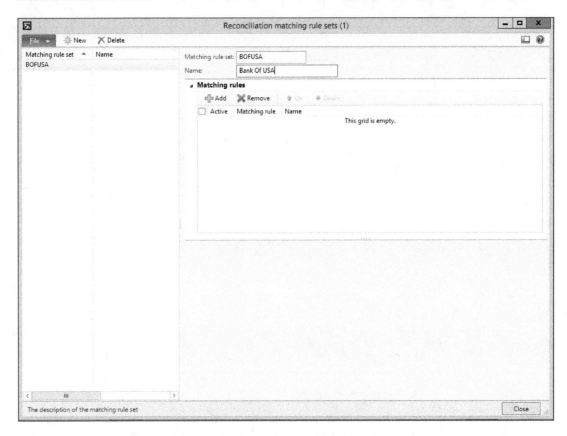

Give your new record a **Matching Rule Set** code and a **Name**. In this example we created a set called BOUSA with a name of Bank Of USA.

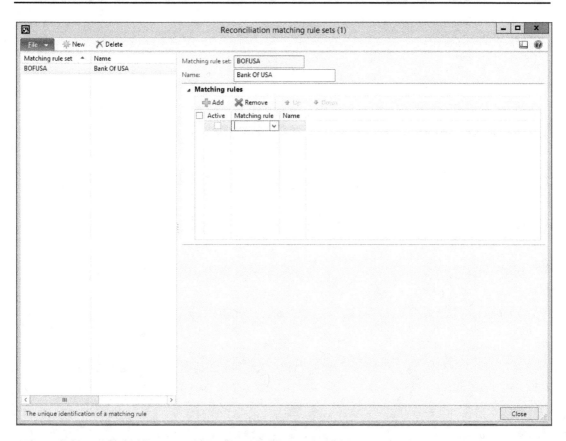

Then click on the **Add** button within the **Matching Rules** tab group.

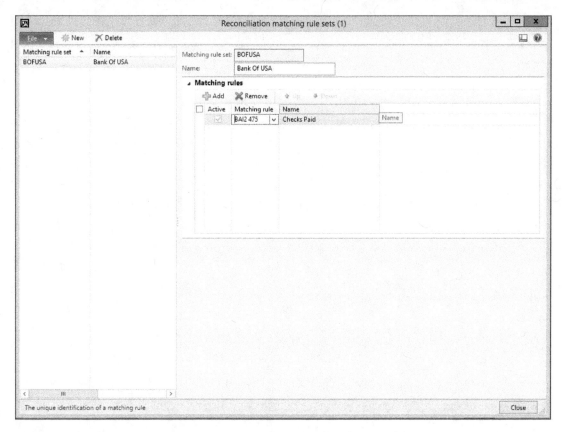

From there select the **Matching Rule** that you want to include in the set.

After you have done that click on the **Close** button to exit from the form.

Performing Automatic Matching

Once you have the Matching Rules and Sets configured you can use them to save yourself a little time.

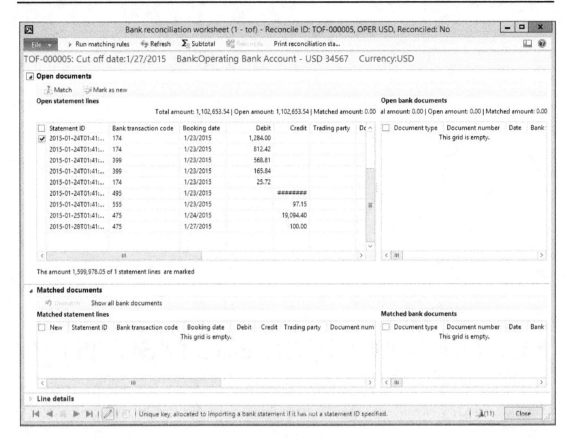

To do this, all you need to do is open up the **Reconciliation Worksheet** form and click on the **Run Matching Rules** button within the menu bar.

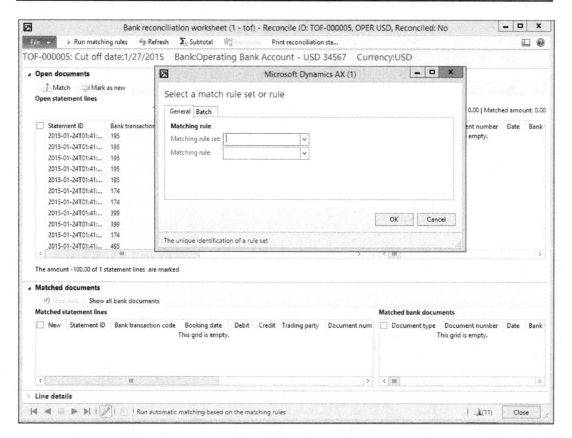

This will open up the **Matching Set or Rule** selection dialog.

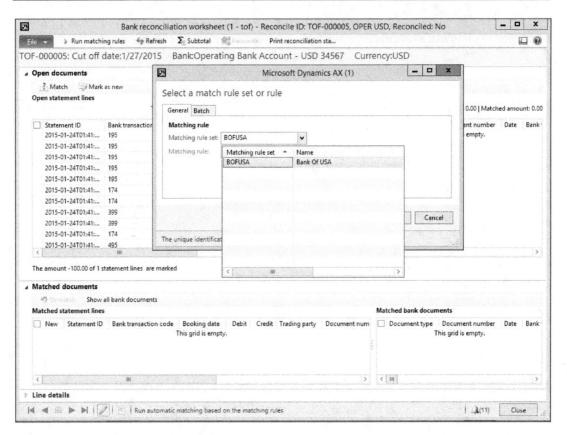

Just select the **Matching Rule** or **Set** that you want to run and click on the **OK** button and let Dynamics AX do all of the hard work for you.

CONFIGRING POSITIVE PAY

One other feature that you might want to configure within the **Cash and Bank Management** area is the Positive Pay feature. This will create the Positive Pay file for you that you can then send to the bank listing out all of the transactions that you have posted within Dynamics AX that are approved to be processed by the bank. The good thing is that this is just a simple configuration step.

Configuring The Positive Pay Outbound Port

In order to enable Positive Pay you need to create and configure the **Positive Pay** outbound port. This may seen like a technical task, but it's not really.

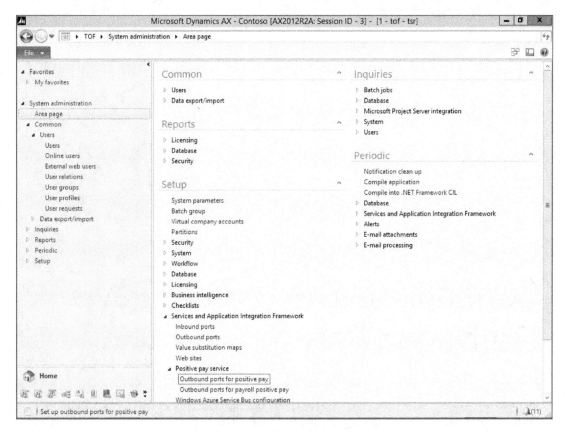

To do this click on the **Outbound Ports for Positive Pay** menu item within the **Positive Pay Service** subfolder of the **Services and Applications Integration Framework** folder within the **Setup** group of the **System Administration** area page.

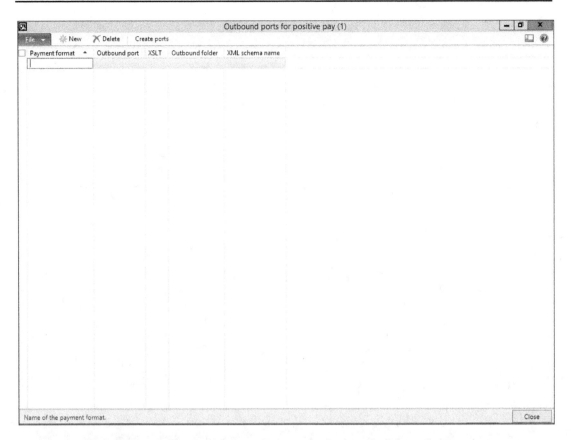

When the **Outbound Ports for Positive Pay** list page is displayed, click on the **New** button to breate a new record.

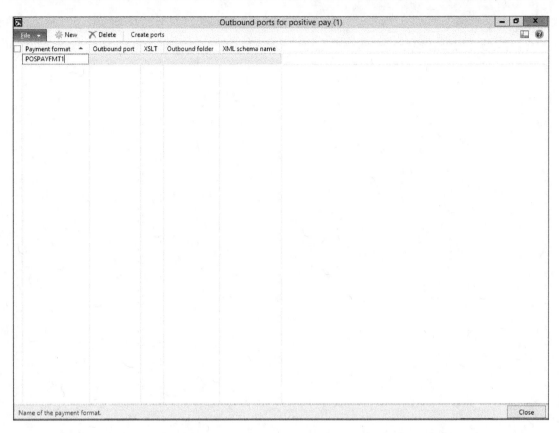

Then type in a name for the **Payment Format**. For this example we will call the format
POSPAYFMT.

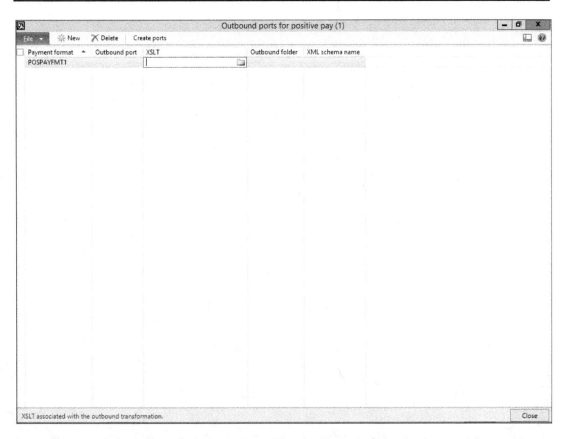

Now we need to find a **XSLT** stylesheet that will be used to transform the data into the positive pay format. To do this click on the folder icon to the right of the **XSLT** field.

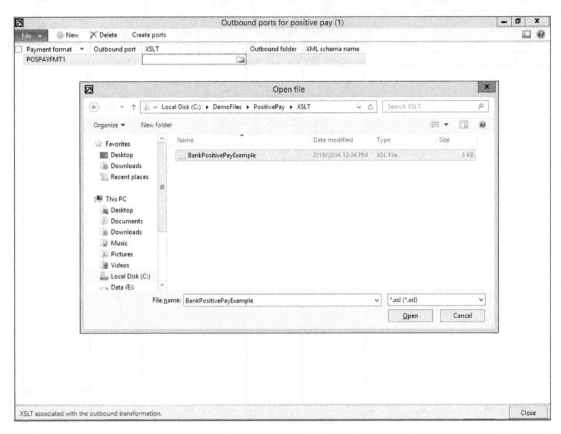

Then the file explorer opens, locate the XSLT file and click the **Open** button.

```xml
<?xml version="1.0" encoding="utf-8"?>
<xsl:stylesheet version="1.0" xmlns:xsl="http://www.w3.org/1999/XSL/Transform"
   xmlns:msxsl="urn:schemas-microsoft-com:xslt" exclude-result-prefixes="msxsl s0 s1 xslthelper" xmlns="urn:iso:std:iso:20022:tech:xsd:pain.001.001.02"
        xmlns:xsi="http://www.w3.org/2001/XMLSchema-instance" xmlns:xslthelper="http://schemas.microsoft.com/BizTalk/2003/xslthelper"
        xmlns:s0="http://schemas.microsoft.com/dynamics/2008/01/sharedtypes"
xmlns:s1="http://schemas.microsoft.com/dynamics/2008/01/documents/BankPositivePay"
        >

 <xsl:template match="/">
  <xsl:apply-templates select="//s1:BankPositivePay"></xsl:apply-templates>
 </xsl:template>
 <xsl:template match="//s1:BankPositivePay">
  <Document>
   <xsl:value-of select="'&#13;&#10;'" />
   <xsl:for-each select="s1:BankAccountTable">
    <xsl:if test="count(child::s1:BankChequeTable) >0">
     <!--Header Begin-->
     <xsl:value-of select='string("Vendor ID,Vendor Name,Voided,Document Type,Check Date,Check Number,Check Amount,Checkbook ID,Vendor Class ID,Posted
Date")'/>
     <xsl:value-of select="'&#13;&#10;'" />
     <!--Header End-->
     <!--Cheque Detail begin-->
     <xsl:for-each select="s1:BankChequeTable">
      <xsl:value-of select='s1:RecipientAccountNum/text()'/>
      <xsl:value-of select="'&#44;'" />
      <xsl:value-of select='s1:BankNegInstRecipientName/text()'/>
      <xsl:value-of select="'&#44;'" />
      <xsl:choose>
       <xsl:when test='s1:ChequeStatus/text()=normalize-space("Void") or s1:ChequeStatus/text()=normalize-space("Rejected") or
s1:ChequeStatus/text()=normalize-space("Cancelled")'>
        <xsl:value-of select='string("Yes")'/>
       </xsl:when>
       <xsl:when test='s1:ChequeStatus/text()=normalize-space("Payment")'>
        <xsl:value-of select='string("No")'/>
       </xsl:when>
       <xsl:otherwise>
        <xsl:value-of select='string(" ")'/>
       </xsl:otherwise>
      </xsl:choose>
      <xsl:value-of select="'&#44;'" />
      <xsl:value-of select='string("Payment")'/>
      <xsl:value-of select="'&#44;'" />
      <xsl:value-of select='s1:TransDate/text()'/>
      <xsl:value-of select="'&#44;'" />
      <xsl:value-of select='s1:ChequeNum/text()'/>
      <xsl:value-of select="'&#44;'" />
      <xsl:value-of select='s1:AmountCur/text()'/>
      <xsl:value-of select="'&#44;'" />
      <xsl:value-of select='string("BOA-#1812")'/>
      <xsl:value-of select="'&#44;'" />
      <xsl:choose>
      <xsl:when test='s1:RecipientType/text()=normalize-space("Vend")'>
      <xsl:for-each select="s1:VendTable">
        <xsl:value-of select='s1:VendGroup/text()'/>
      </xsl:for-each>
      </xsl:when>
      <xsl:otherwise>
        <xsl:for-each select="s1:CustTable">
         <xsl:value-of select='s1:CustGroup/text()'/>
        </xsl:for-each>
       </xsl:otherwise>
      </xsl:choose>
      <xsl:value-of select="'&#44;'" />
      <xsl:value-of select='s1:TransDate/text()'/>
      <xsl:value-of select="'&#13;&#10;'" />
     </xsl:for-each>
    </xsl:if>
   </xsl:for-each>
  </Document>
 </xsl:template>
```

```
<msxsl:script language="C#" implements-prefix="xslthelper">
  <![CDATA[
  public string PadLeft(string value,int length,string paddingchar)
  {
   if(paddingchar!=String.Empty)
   {
    return value.PadLeft(length,(paddingchar.ToCharArray())[0]);
    }
    else
    {
     return value.PadLeft(length);
    }
  }
  public string FormatDate(string date)
  {
   DateTime dateTime=DateTime.Parse(date);
   if(dateTime!=null)
   {
   return dateTime.ToString("MMddyyyy");
   }
   else
   {
   return String.Empty;
   }

  }
  public int ConvertToInt(string s)
  {
   Double f=Convert.ToDouble(s);
   return (int)f;
  }
]]>
 </msxsl:script>
</xsl:stylesheet>
```

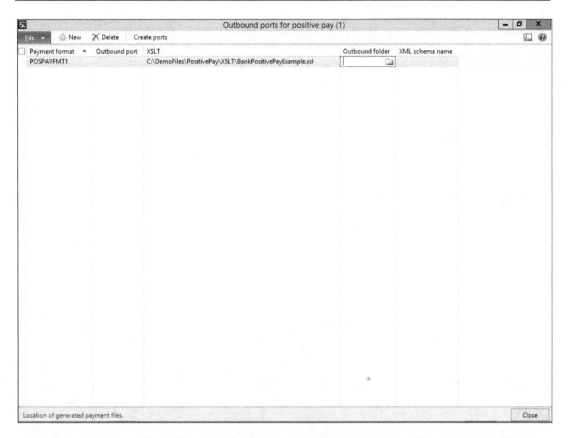

Next we need to specify a folder that the Positive Pay file is to be dropped in. To do this click on the folder icon to the right of the **Outbound Folder** field.

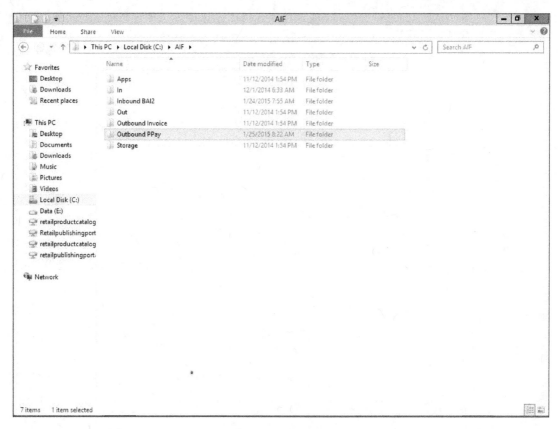

Tip: We just created a file folder of the **Outbound Ppay** in the AIF folder.

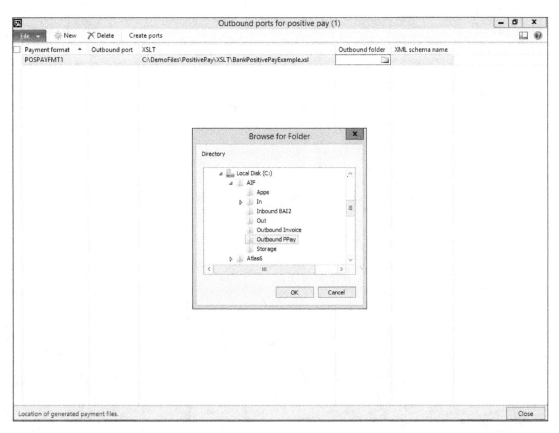

Then the folder explorer opens, locate the folder that you created for the positive pay file and click the **OK** button.

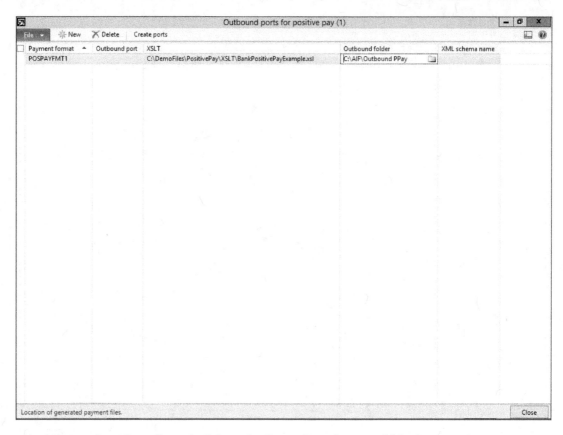

Now that we have it configured, click on the **Create Ports** button within the menu bar to create the AIF ports.

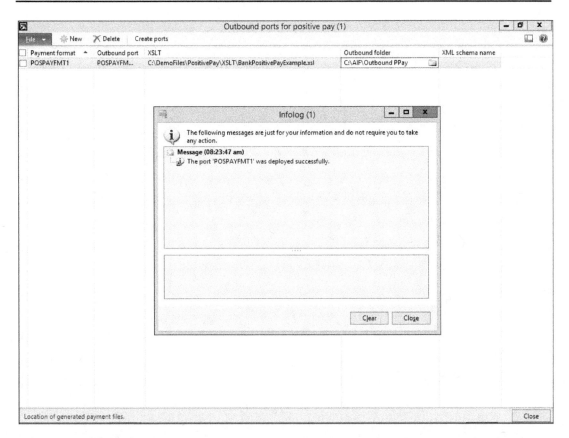

If everything is find then you will get a note saying that the ports have been created and you can exit from the InfoLog.

Tweaking the Positive Pay Outbound Port

Although Dynamics AX has created the Outbound Port for you, it might be a good idea to make a few tweaks to it.

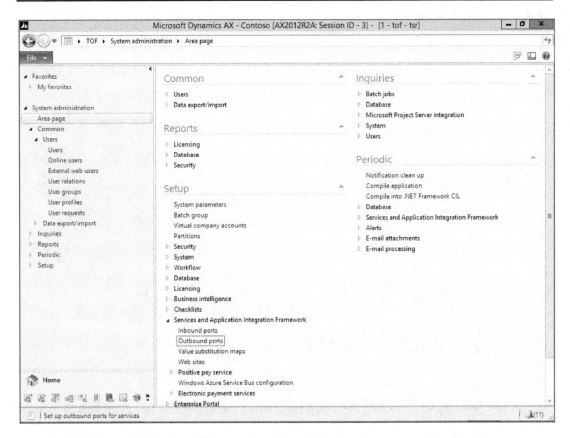

To do this click on the **Outbound Ports** menu item within the **Services and Applications Integration Framework** folder within the **Setup** group of the **System Administration** area page.

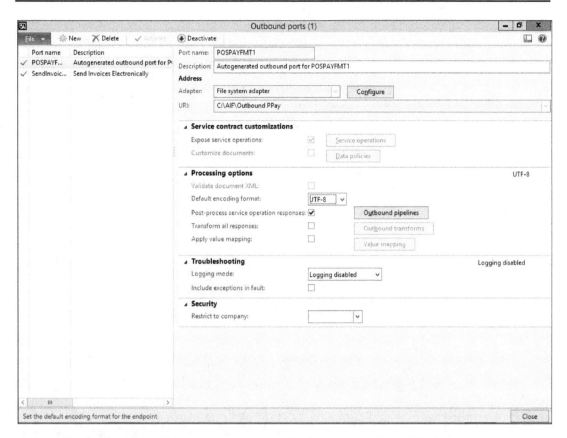

When the **Outbound Ports** maintenance form is displayed you will see that there is a new port for your **POSPAYFMT** port.

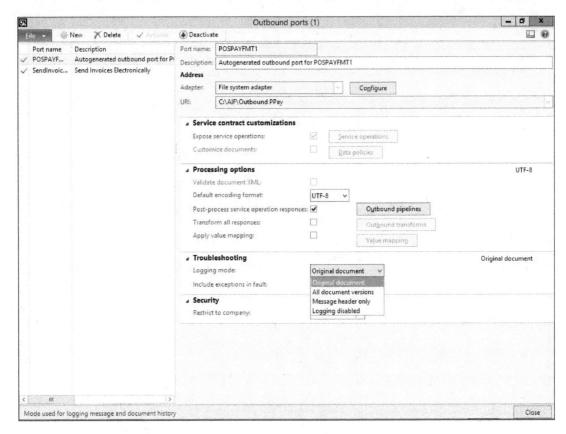

Change the **Logging Mode** field to **Original Document**.

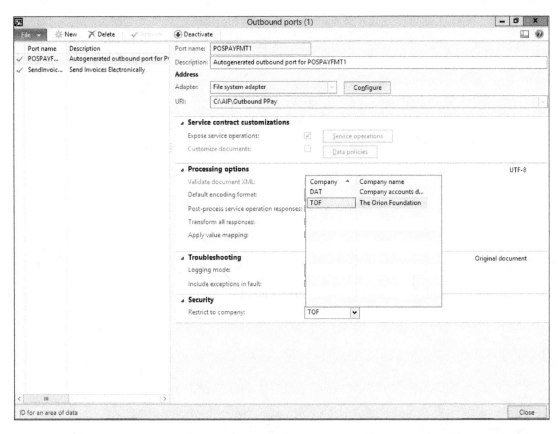

And then if you want to secure down the port a little more you can also click on the **Restrict To Company** field and select the company that you want this port to be run against.

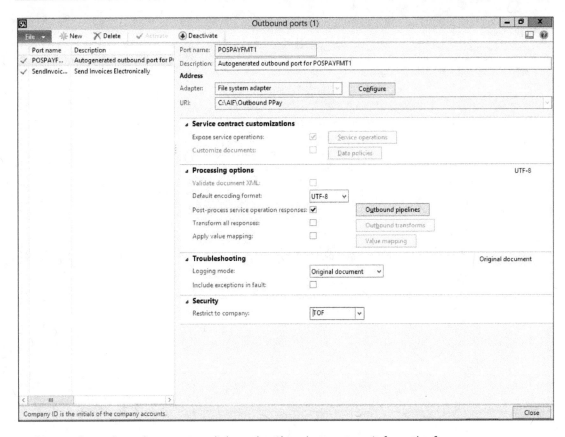

After you have done that you can click on the **Close** button to exit from the form.

Creating The Positive Pay File

Now that you have configured the Positive Pay Ports you can start using them.

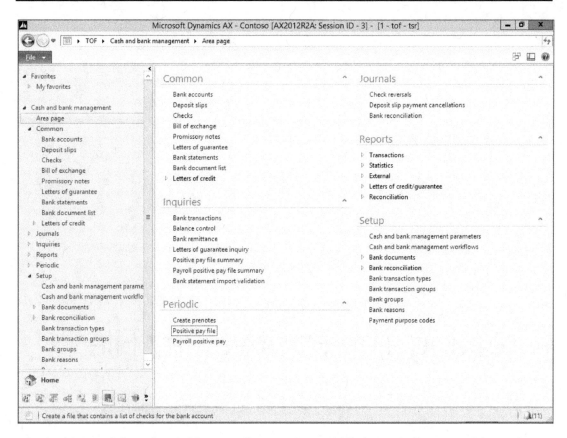

To do this just click on the **Positive Pay File** menu item within the **Periodic** group of the **Cash and Bank Management** area page.

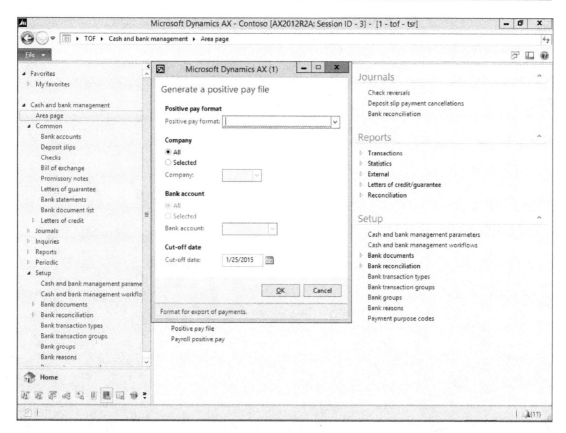

This will open up the **Generate A Positive Pay File** dialog box.

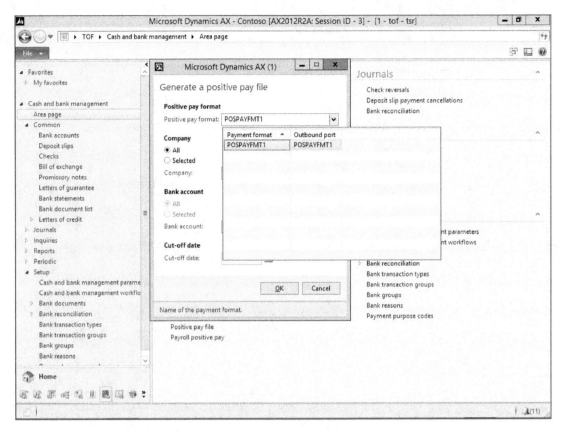

Click on the **Positive Pay Format** dropdown list select the format code that you juct configured.

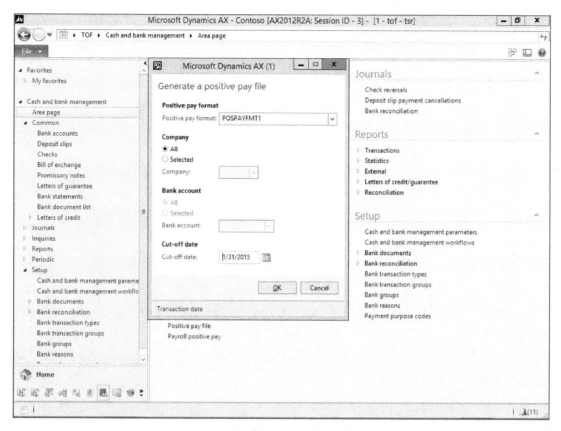

You can change the **Cut Off Date** if you like and when you are ready just click on the **OK** button.

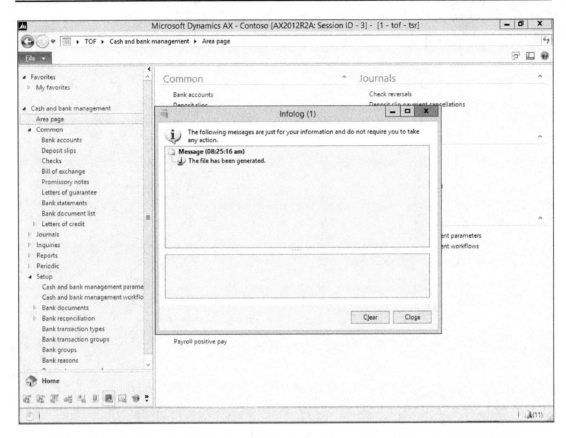

You will get a notice that the Positive Pay file has been generated and if you look in the AIF folder that you assigned to the format then you should find it there.

How easy is that?

SUMMARY

Now you have the base **Cash And Bank Management** configuration completed. All that is left to do is to start getting the money in and spending it.

Want More Tips & Tricks For Dynamics AX?

The Tips & Tricks series is a compilation of all the cool things that I have found that you can do within Dynamics AX, and are also the basis for my Tips & Tricks presentations that I have been giving for the AXUG, and online. Unfortunately book page size restrictions mean that I can only fit 50 tips & tricks per book, but I will create new volumes every time I reach the 50 Tip mark.

To get all of the details on this series, then here is the link:

http://dynamicsaxcompanions.com/tipsandtricks

Need More Help With Dynamics AX?

LUKE SKYWALKER MAY HAVE HAD THE FORCE,
BUT HE STILL NEEDED R2D2 TO PLOT THE
COURSE FOR HIM.
WHO IS YOUR COMPANION THAT WILL HELP YOU
NAVIGATE DYNAMICS AX?

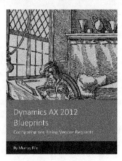

After creating a number of my walkthroughs on SlideShare showing how to configure the different areas within Dynamics AX, I had a lot of requests for the original documents so that people could get a better view of many of the screen shots and also have a easy reference as they worked through the same process within their own systems. To make them easier to access, I am in the process of moving all of the content to the Dynamics AX Companions website to easier access. If you are looking for details on how to configure and use Dynamics AX, then this is a great place for you to start.

Here is the link for the site:

http://dynamicsaxcompanions.com/

About Me

I am an author - I'm no Dan Brown but my books do contain a lot of secret codes and symbols that help guide you through the mysteries of Dynamics AX.

I am a curator - gathering all of the information that I can about Dynamics AX and filing it away within the Dynamics AX Companions archives.

I am a pitchman - I am forever extolling the virtues of Dynamics AX to the unwashed masses convincing them that it is the best ERP system in the world.

I am a Microsoft MVP - this is a big deal, there are less than 10 Dynamics AX MVP's in the US, and less than 30 worldwide.

I am a programmer - I know enough to get around within code, although I leave the hard stuff to the experts so save you all from my uncommented style.

WEB	**www.**murrayfife.me
EMAIL	murray@dynamicsaxcompanions.com
TWITTER	@murrayfife
SKYPE	murrayfife
AMAZON	www.amazon.com/author/murrayfife
WEB	www.dynamicsaxcompanions.com

www.ingramcontent.com/pod-product-compliance
Lightning Source LLC
LaVergne TN
LVHW062301060326
832902LV00013B/2004